THE RED VELVET CAKE WAR

BY **JESSIE JONES**
NICHOLAS HOPE
JAMIE WOOTEN

★

★

DRAMATISTS
PLAY SERVICE
INC.

THE RED VELVET CAKE WAR
Copyright © 2010, Jessie Jones, Nicholas Hope, Jamie Wooten

All Rights Reserved

We dedicate this play to Winkie Lee,
accomplished journalist and dear friend.

AUTHORS' NOTES

The roles of Grover and Purvis can be doubled, as can the roles of Cee Cee and Mama Doll.

Gaynelle's living room is the only set. All other locations should be suggested by lighting.

We strongly suggest all action involving Newt Blaylock's prosthetic eyeball be mimed.

We also suggest up-tempo music be played pre- and post-show, at intermission and especially during scene transitions.

The characters who populate Sweetgum, Texas, should be portrayed as real people, not Southern caricatures.

All of the characters portrayed in *The Red Velvet Cake War* are fictional creations, and any resemblance to real persons, living or dead, is purely coincidental.

THE RED VELVET CAKE WAR received its world premiere at Johnson City Community Theatre in Johnson City, Tennessee, on October 8, 2010. It was directed by Joe Smith; the assistant director was Shannon Skinner; the scenic design was by Kaeli Gardner; the costume design was by Linda Wakely; the hair/wig supervision was by Jayme Hill; the makeup design was by Derek Smithpeters; the lighting and sound design were by April Gardner and Eric Hyche; and the stage manager was Colleen Dunne. The cast was as follows:

CEE CEE WINDHAM	Sabra Hayden
GAYNELLE VERDEEN BODEEN	Debbie Shoun
LA MERLE VERDEEN MINSHEW	Jean Bashor
AUBREY VERDEEN	Steve Bashor
JIMMIE WYVETTE VERDEEN	Donna Deason
PEACHES VERDEEN BELROSE	Joy Nagy
BITSY HARGIS	Vicky Livesay
NEWT BLAYLOCK	Larry Bunton
SHERIFF GROVER LOUT	Aaron Bradley
ELSA DOWDALL	Angie Hyche
MAMA DOLL HARGIS	Betty Casey
PURVIS VERDEEN	Jeff Light

THE RED VELVET CAKE WAR received its Southwest Regional premiere at Theatre Off The Square in Weatherford, Texas, on that same evening, October 8, 2010. It was directed by Jon R. Kruse; the scenic design was by Chuck Hudson; the costume design was by Debby Herbel; the lighting and sound design were by Nikolai Braswell and Wally Jones; and the stage managers were Debby Herbel and Melissa Teague. The cast was as follows:

CEE CEE WINDHAM .... Laurie Jones
GAYNELLE VERDEEN BODEEN .... Cynthia Daniels
LA MERLE VERDEEN MINSHEW .... Joyce Eckstein
AUBREY VERDEEN .... Duncan Alexander
JIMMIE WYVETTE VERDEEN .... Catherine Wise
PEACHES VERDEEN BELROSE .... Peggy Osburn
BITSY HARGIS .... Karen Dohoney
NEWT BLAYLOCK .... Ray Shannon
SHERIFF GROVER LOUT .... Wally Jones
ELSA DOWDALL .... Cynthia Sadler
MAMA DOLL HARGIS .... Darlene Woodruff
PURVIS VERDEEN .... Jordan Nissen

CHARACTERS
(in order of appearance)

Freda CEE CEE WINDHAM, late 40s to 50

Melanie GAYNELLE VERDEEN BODEEN, late 40s

JoAnn LAMERLE VERDEEN MINSHEW, late 60s to 70

Chuck AUBREY VERDEEN, late 80s

Carrie JIMMIE WYVETTE VERDEEN, 40s

Heather PEACHES VERDEEN BELROSE, late 40s

Paige BITSY HARGIS, late 40s

Terry NEWT BLAYLOCK, 50s

JW SHERIFF GROVER LOUT, 50s

Kristine ELSA DOWDALL, 40s to 50s

Terry MAMA DOLL HARGIS, 80s to 120

JW PURVIS VERDEEN, 50s to 60s

Trina stage manager
Marsha Photos
Joel lighting

PLACE

In and around the home Gaynelle Verdeen Bodeen,
Sweetgum, Texas, USA.

TIME

The present.

ACT ONE

Scene 1: Thursday morning, mid-July

Scene 2: A few minutes later

Scene 3: Moments later

Scene 4: Seconds later

>**Scene 5:** That afternoon

Scene 6: Friday evening

>**Scene 7:** Early Saturday morning

ACT TWO

Scene 1: Later that morning

>**Scene 2:** One hour later

>**Scene 3:** That afternoon

Scene 4: One hour later

THE RED VELVET CAKE WAR

ACT ONE

Scene 1

Monday Thursday morning [handwritten annotation]

Morning, mid-July, lights up center stage on a small counter-top, the "set" of Hospitality House, *a low-budget cable access program in Sweetgum, Texas. Cee Cee Windham, sassy and stylish, addresses "the camera."*

CEE CEE. Hi, everybody! I'm Cee Cee Windham, your hostess here on *Hospitality House,* the number-one cable access show in the tri-county area. As you know, Thursday means a visit to our What-Me-Not Workbench, where we'll create a craft that is nothing but C.D.P. — cute, darlin' and precious! But first, let's check out this week's calendar of exciting cultural events in Sweetgum to see what's going on. *(Picks up a blank piece of paper, checks both sides.)* Well, not much. Now, our guest today is none other than my very best friend. We're celebrating the good news that those pesky charges of attempted murder filed against her by her newly *ex*-husband and his *lady friend* have been dismissed! So, now that she's not being sent up to the big house, let's give a good ol' Texas howdy to Gaynelle Verdeen Bodeen! *(Canned music plays as Gaynelle Verdeen Bodeen, late 40s, a walking nervous breakdown, enters and tentatively joins Cee Cee behind the counter.)* Gaynelle, we haven't seen much of you since the *unfortunate incident.* Anything you'd like to say to all your friends and neighbors who've missed you so much? *(No answer. Gaynelle stares terrified at "the camera.")* Gaynelle? *(Elbows her.)*

GAYNELLE. *(Shouts.)* NOT GUILTY!

CEE CEE. *(Into "the camera.")* Two of the sweetest words in the English language. *(Gaynelle slowly sinks out of view. Without missing a beat, Cee Cee pulls her back up by the collar.)* Now, Gaynelle, I know you're ready to get crafty. Here's a mat for a photograph we're going to dress up with various doo-dads. So, let's just hit the back of it with every gal's favorite weapon, the hot glue gun! *(Does so.)* Now, what would you like to do with this little heart?

GAYNELLE. *(Fixates on the heart.)* Oh, I'll tell you what I'd like to do with it! *(Snatches the heart, puts it on the mat, pounds it.)* I'd like to pound that sucker until it's flatter than roadkill, just like *Sumner* did to mine! *(Increasingly fervent.)* Then grind it into the ground and just see how *he* likes it! Yeah! Let's pound and grind and pound and grind for twenty-seven long, wasted years until you think you can't take it anymore! Yes, yes, yes! *(Bursts into tears, runs offstage.)*

CEE CEE. *(Covers, speaks into "the camera.")* See how easy it is to lose yourself to the passion of craftin'? So, while I finish up, let's hear from our sponsor, Travis Ponder's Bible and Tire Outlet, where they're running a special, "*KJV* Plus Three." Buy three belted radials and get a free leatherette copy of the Good Book. Folks, that's a deal, unless you're a big fan of Second Thessalonians, which was accidentally printed upside down … *and* in Korean. But it's not one of the biggies, so you probably won't miss it. Now, y'all run grab you another cuppa and we'll be right back, live, from Sweetgum, Texas! *(Blackout.)*

Scene 2 *Monday*

A few minutes later. Lights up stage right on LaMerle Verdeen Minshew, the well-dressed, self-serving, sharp-tongued matriarch of the Verdeen clan. She serves lunch to her Uncle Aubrey Verdeen, the good-natured, oxygen-dependent patriarch of the family, who wears a nasal cannula attached to his ever-present oxygen tank on wheels. Dressed in a suit and string tie, he sits at a table in his "kitchen." Nearby is a shopping bag and an opened purse. LaMerle and Aubrey have been one-upping each other for decades.

AUBREY. Hey, LaMerle, did you hear scientists identified a food that can diminish a man's sex drive by ninety percent? It's called wedding cake! *(Cackles.)*

LA MERLE. *(Gives him a cool stare.)* Isn't it a little early in the day to dive into the gutter? I expect that kind of filth from the less evolved members of the family, but not from you. Mark my words, Uncle Aubrey, because of Gaynelle's recent escapades, the eyes of Texas are upon us. So I say we stay on our best behavior 'til this latest public humiliation blows over.

AUBREY. Shoot, LaMerle, this family's endured worse. Now, where's the eats?

LA MERLE. We Verdeens have held our heads up high in Sweetgum for generations. It does not sit well with me that our sterling reputation has been tarnished on *my* watch. *(Pulls a covered plate from the shopping bag. Aubrey eyes it hungrily throughout the following.)* I've spent years fighting to pull the lesser Verdeens up the ladder of society, but clearly, I'm losing the battle with those three cousins. Peaches drove her man off and is squatting in an RV, Jimmie Wyvette gives a whole new definition to "peculiar" and Gaynelle ... well, I can't add more than what's been printed in the police blotter. I'm telling you, those three are a freak show without a tent. *(Sets the plate down.)*

AUBREY. Turnips?! I'm not eating 'em! Turnips are a mistake of nature. Even God knew He blew it with turnips, that's why He buried the durned things!

LA MERLE. Yeah? Well, I dug 'em up and you're eating 'em.

AUBREY. Woman, your heart is colder than a cast-iron commode. Have you been this evil all your life?

LA MERLE. Not yet! Now I have some important news to share.

AUBREY. What, you've been named high priestess of your coven?

LA MERLE. *(Ignores him.)* I've cancelled the Verdeen family reunion Saturday. It's for the greater good. Maybe this time next year, Gaynelle's scandal won't be such juicy fodder for town gossips. So the reunion's cancelled. Period. Now you can either agree with me or you can be wrong.

AUBREY. You can't do that! We're gonna celebrate my ninetieth birthday at the reunion. No, ma'am! I won't stand for this! There's no way I —

LA MERLE. *(Calmly takes a handful of Aubrey's oxygen tube, gives it a good twist, cutting off the air flow.)* Me, me, me, me, me! Couldn't you muster the decency to think of someone else for once and just hang on 'til your ninety-first?! We'll celebrate it *then*, for heaven's sake. Now, clean up those turnips! *(Releases the tube; Aubrey immediately recovers. She turns away. During the following, unseen, Aubrey scrapes the turnips into LaMerle's purse.)* Now, I've got to get my hair fixed, run my Caddy through the car wash and stop by the mini-mart. See you tomorrow. *(Kisses the top of his head, picks up her purse.)* Yes, sir, this family tree could use a good pruning. *(Exits stage right.)*

AUBREY. And she's just the old prune to do it! *(Cackles with glee, then reaches into a pocket and pulls out a Moon Pie, unwraps it. Blackout.)*

Scene 3

Monday

Moments later. Lights up stage left on the "break room" at Whatley's Western Wear. Jimmie Wyvette Verdeen, a hearty good ol' girl with an unfortunate unibrow, dressed in classic mens' Western wear, stands at a table, her foot on a chair, gives her boot a spit shine with a cloth. Peaches Verdeen Belrose, a loud-talking, fun-loving flashy dresser, rushes in stage left, with a small shopping bag.

PEACHES. Jimmie Wyvette! Feels like months since we've seen each other! *(They hug.)* Sorry I'm late, baby cousin, but I was called in on an emergency.

JIMMIE WYVETTE. How do you do it, Peaches? On the road every day, driving all over in that RV, making your clients all look their very best. You are a true artist.

PEACHES. It's a noble, but lonely calling being the number-one mortuarial cosmetologist in this part of the state. But bringing beauty to the bereaved is my destiny. And it's well worth it now that so many folks are requesting me to do makeup and hair for their dearly departed. I guess you could say people are just *dyin'* to hire me! *(Laughs. Then.)* You sure I'm not interfering with your work?

JIMMIE WYVETTE. No, after twenty-three years here at Whatley's Western Wear, I call my own shots.

PEACHES. *(Pulls makeup from the shopping bag.)* Well, thanks for taking time to see me. Say, would you mind letting me try this makeup on you while we talk? They didn't have my usual brand, so I bought this and need to see how it goes on.

JIMMIE WYVETTE. Uh ... I'm not a big fan of makeup but—

PEACHES. Thanks, precious. *(Applies foundation to Jimmie Wyvette's face.)* Now, reason I had to talk to you is this: You heard Aunt LaMerle cancelled the Verdeen family reunion?

JIMMIE WYVETTE. *(Flinches as Peaches works.)* Yeah, talk about a relief.

PEACHES. Shug, we're *un-cancelling* it, Gaynelle's gonna host the reunion and you and me are gonna help her do it.

13

JIMMIE WYVETTE. But I'm workin' the Little Britches Calf Scramble Saturday.

PEACHES. Well, we're just gonna have to put our selfish pursuits aside. The three of us have always been there for each other in tough times ... even though Gaynelle's taken it to a whole new level trying to kill her husband's girlfriend.

JIMMIE WYVETTE. *Ex*-husband. And Gaynelle told us she blacked out before she hit that speed bump and crashed through the wall of Rabeena Sadler's doublewide. It was an accident.

PEACHES. Yeah, but as Gaynelle's minivan hurtled across the lawn, Rabeena's neighbor swore she heard someone hollering, "Remember the Alamo!"

JIMMIE WYVETTE. Strictly hearsay. Anyway, Judge Wardlow believed Gaynelle. *(Beat.)* Okay, maybe he didn't, but at that point I think he would've done anything to get her out of his courtroom to stop the wailing and projectile vomiting.

PEACHES. Yeah, Gaynelle lucked out on that. But Sumner's fancy lawyer insisted Gaynelle pass a psychological exam and if she blows it, they'll send her straight to the loony bin. So, our job is to make sure our cousin passes that evaluation. *(Studies her work.)* Say, this makeup looks good!

JIMMIE WYVETTE. No fooling? Maybe I ought to get some. What kind is it?

PEACHES. Eternally Beautiful. And the shade is Death Becomes Her.

JIMMIE WYVETTE. *(Panics.)* Dead people's makeup?!

PEACHES. Relax! It's the same stuff you get in the drugstore, just thicker.

JIMMIE WYVETTE. Get it off! Now! Now! *(Wipes at her face with her boot shine rag.)* I don't know which one I hate worse, having to go to a Verdeen family reunion or wearing cadaver cosmetics. Did you drop by just to torture me?

PEACHES. *(Takes Jimmie Wyvette by the shoulders.)* Listen to me. I found out that Gaynelle's evaluation is going to happen *this weekend* but we're not supposed to know it! What's worse, the psychologist assigned to the case is Elsa Dowdall, the toughest one around. But she's bound to give Gaynelle a passing grade and let her go free if she sees Gaynelle successfully handling a big get-together and interacting with a normal, loving family.

JIMMIE WYVETTE. Wait. Where are *we* gonna find a *normal, lov-*

ing family? (Off Peaches' look.) Alright, I'm in. Poor Gaynelle. Hard to believe Rabeena Sadler actually stole Sumner away from her. No wonder she resorted to vehicular violence.

PEACHES. Yeah, guess it's true what Great-Uncle Aubrey's always spouting: You have two choices in life — you can stay single and be miserable …

PEACHES/JIMMIE WYVETTE. … Or get married and wish you were dead! *(They laugh. Blackout.)*

Scene 4 ~Monday~

Seconds later. Lights up center stage on the Hospitality House *"set." A large Mason jar filled with folded slips of paper is on the countertop. Unaware the camera is rolling, Cee Cee tries to encourage Gaynelle.*

CEE CEE. … I'm just saying, you've got to get a grip. Doing things like being on my show can help you reclaim your place in this community. From now on, you've got to walk proud. Even though your husband dumped you for someone younger and prettier, you have got to hold your head up high.

GAYNELLE. But I just feel like I've been stomped on and thrown in the bar ditch. I don't know if I can go on.

CEE CEE. Of course you can! That's what Texas women do. We keep a-goin'!

GAYNELLE. *(Realizes the camera is running.)* Uh… are we back on the —

CEE CEE. *(Unaware the camera's on.)* You think there aren't days I feel like hell? But do I let it get me down? No ma'am! I *go on,* Gaynelle. You know who my viewers are? Homely gals with thighs the size of tree stumps and trailer trash who think "formal wear" means a clean tank top. They're all counting on me. And even if I feel like I'd rather put a gun to my head than face another recipe using cream of mushroom soup, I do it. I stand up in front of that camera and *fake it.* And you have to do the same, because you — *(Glances at "the camera," quickly covers.)* Well, looks like we're back …

without a warning from Harley, our cameraman, or anything! Now, before we leave these thirty minutes of gracious living behind, we always answer one question about etiquette. Gaynelle, do the honors and fish me out a question from our Good Manners Mason jar. *(Gaynelle pulls a slip of paper from the jar.)*

GAYNELLE. *(Reads.)* "Cee Cee, what two things should a lady never do in bed?"

CEE CEE. Why, girl, that's easy! *Point* and *laugh!* *(Laughs.)* Good-bye everybody! See you next time here on *Hospitality House!* *(Blackout.)*

Scene 5   *Monday*

Thursday

That afternoon. Lights up center stage on Gaynelle's living room in her comfortable Texas Victorian home. An upstage left door leads to the kitchen. A dining table and chairs sit just downstage of the kitchen door. The front door is downstage right and a downstage left hallway door leads to the rest of the house. A buffet is on the stage right wall. Downstage center are a couch and arm chair. Peaches and Jimmie Wyvette sip coffee on the couch.

JIMMIE WYVETTE. You ever find living in an RV kinda claustrophobic?

PEACHES. Oh, no. There are so many advantages, like an ever-changing panorama and, no matter where you go, you've got all your stuff with you. It's like a mobile purse with a microwave. *(Gaynelle bursts through the kitchen door.)*

GAYNELLE. *(Rants as she hurriedly paces the room. Peaches and Jimmie Wyvette do not react.)* And after all I've been through, you're telling me I *have* to host the family reunion?! I mean, haven't I suffered enough? Well, I'm not doing it and that's that! *(Exits into the kitchen. Beat.)*

PEACHES. And, too, with an RV, there's no yard to mow.

JIMMIE WYVETTE. That *is* a big plus.

GAYNELLE. *(Bursts through the kitchen door, rages.)* This is an awful time for me and that psychologist will just have to wait!

16

(Beelines back to the kitchen door.) No, ma'am, I do not agree! So, put a stop to it right now! *(Exits into the kitchen.)*

PEACHES.   You know, Gaynelle's taking it a lot better than I thought she would.

JIMMIE WYVETTE.   She really is. *(Sips her coffee.)*

GAYNELLE.   *(Bursts through the kitchen door.)* And in case you've been vacationing on Pluto, may I remind you my reputation's ruined and I've been ridiculed all over this town. *(Pulls a can of whipped cream from her pocket.)* Do you honestly believe I want to get the Verdeens together so they can have another shot at me, too? *(Squirts cream into her mouth.)* You must think I'm crazy!

PEACHES.   No, *we* don't, shug. *(Puts an arm around her.)* But your ex-husband *does*. Face it, Gaynelle, Sumner wants his revenge!

GAYNELLE.   Seems to me him having an affair, slapping me with a quick-y divorce and cleaning out our bank accounts before I even knew what hit me, is *plenty!* When do I get *my* revenge?

JIMMIE WYVETTE.   Well, there's a rap sheet with your name on it that says you're off to a pretty good start.

GAYNELLE.   *(Misty.)* How did my life fall apart?! I was president of the Lone Star Ladies Book Club. I volunteered at the Sweetgum City Museum, every third Tuesday, ten to three. I was Mrs. Sumner Bodeen. *(Takes a hit of cream.)* You'd think a fifty-year-old CPA would have a *normal* mid-life crisis like every other man. But no! Instead of getting a red sports car, Sumner got him a tacky little redhead from over at the Dollar General in Fayro.

PEACHES.   *(Takes the whipped cream.)* Come on, now. Where's the Gaynelle we used to know? That fighter who never let anyone get the best of her.

GAYNELLE.   She *died*. So have some respect. Lord, this all makes me just want to drop off the face of the earth like Rex did.

JIMMIE WYVETTE.   Uh, speaking of which, you haven't heard from that husband of yours or anything, have you, Peaches?

PEACHES.   Of course not. When he crawled into his big rig that night all those years ago, that was the last I saw of Theodore Rexford Belrose. If I'd known, I would've hollered, "I'll love you forever" instead of "Bring home a jumbo pack of Charmin, we're down to the last four sheets!" *(Teary.)* To this day I still get choked up every time I change the toilet paper roll.

JIMMIE WYVETTE.   Well, that *is* a good time to reminisce.

PEACHES.   For years, I never gave up hope. A buddy called, said he thought he spotted T. Rex's truck in Anchorage; a few years later, someone said he *might've* seen him in Pensacola. With all these sightings, I feel like I've been married to Bigfoot! *(Then.)* Oh, heck. I hadn't wanted to bring this up today, but since we're all talking about it, maybe it *is* the right time. *(Pulls a manila envelope from her purse.)* But I ought to warn you, this might seem a little strange.

GAYNELLE. Strange?! Peaches, at this low point in my life, I can honestly say there's nothing strange that I can't handle. *(Bitsy Hargis, perky, prim, nosy and a throwback to the 1950s, enters the front door.)*

BITSY. Knockety-knock-knock! Everybody decent?

GAYNELLE. *(Low.)* I take it back. *(Grabs the can of cream, takes a hit.)*

PEACHES. *(Shoves the papers into her purse.)* We'll talk about this later.

BITSY. Gaynelle, you poor thing! Mama Doll got so tickled watching you on the TV today she spit her upper plate across the kitchen table. I came over because I saw your RV in the drive, Peaches, and I need an expert: Is my eyeliner too thick? I mean, how do I look?

PEACHES. Well, you look … like … you always do.

BITSY. That's so sweet of you to say! I do want to look nice when I deliver my tamale pie over to Burton Pearsol. He's taken a real shine to me. *(Jimmie Wyvette slams her fist down on the table.)*

JIMMIE WYVETTE. *(Rising temper.)* Burton's wife's only been gone a few days. Don't you think he needs a little time to grieve?

BITSY. I'm only being neighborly, Jimmie Wy. Well, gotta run. *(Crosses to the front door.)* I promised to walk Trinket, Burton's Great Dane. Oh, if Mama Doll wanders over, just hide the cooking sherry, make sure she's not wearing that bra on her head and aim her back toward the house. Bye-dee-bye-bye! *(Exits the front door.)*

JIMMIE WYVETTE. That burns me up, Bitsy throwing herself at Burton!

GAYNELLE. She *is* moving mighty fast on a new widower.

JIMMIE WYVETTE. I don't mean *that*. I mean, I've got *my* eye on him.

PEACHES. *(Exchanges a look with Gaynelle.)* Why, darlin', this is a new development! We've never known you to be interested in anyone since the tragic accident with the rodeo clown.

JIMMIE WYVETTE. I never should've thrown Buckles a kiss at the same time that bull came out of the chute. Oh, well, live and learn.

GAYNELLE. You can't go chasing Burton so soon after Lurlene's death. It's just not good manners.

PEACHES. Gaynelle, sometimes good manners have to give way to *good sense*. After the age of fifty, the ratio of men to women becomes dangerously unbalanced and an eligible male becomes a hot commodity. It's a known fact that once a man's been married, he's incapable of living alone. So, if he loses his wife, he's gonna turn to the first woman who grabs his attention. Trust me, a widower's fair game the minute the dirt hits his wife's casket.

JIMMIE WYVETTE. So if all these women are going to be after Burton, how do I compete with 'em?

PEACHES. By seizing grief by the horns and trusting a professional. Now, get the tweezers out of my purse and I'll start on your eyebrows.

JIMMIE WYVETTE. Uh ...what's wrong with my eyebrows?

PEACHES. Well, shug, traditionally, a woman has *two*. *(To Gaynelle.)* And now that we're taking care of Jimmie Wyvette's little problem ... *(Grabs the can of cream.)* we're gonna tackle *yours*.

GAYNELLE. Nooo! It helps me cope. Some people smoke, some drink, I squirt whipped cream. It's my *friend! (Grabs the can.)*

PEACHES. It's a crutch and it's gotta go! *(Snatches the can back.)*

GAYNELLE. You're not taking my high-fructose-corn-syrup-sodium-polyphosphate-aerosol-dessert-topping away! Give it to me! Now, now, now!

PEACHES. *(To Jimmie Wyvette.)* It's always hard seeing someone's ugly side. *(LaMerle storms in the front door.)*

LA MERLE. *(With disdain.)* Well, you three have done it again!

PEACHES. *(To Jimmie Wyvette.)* See? It never gets any easier.

LA MERLE. *(Fumes.)* Just when I cancel the Verdeen reunion, you three take it upon yourselves to say we're having it *anyway?!* I swear, y'all have been a blight on our good family name since you got old enough to shave your legs. *(To Jimmie Wyvette.)* Which I strongly suggest should be done more than once a year. *(To Peaches.)* And you! Flip-tailing around, looking like you've been poured into your clothes and forgot to say "when." *(To Gaynelle.)* And it's become painfully clear *your* mental state's about as steady as a pig on ice!

GAYNELLE. Good to see you, too, Aunt LaMerle.

LA MERLE. *(Ignores her.)* Gaynelle, you've dragged our entire family through the sludge of your life and the only decent, Christian thing we can do now is lay low and hope folks find another idiot to talk about.

JIMMIE WYVETTE. Actually, Aunt LaMerle, we thought it's time those of us in the … uh … younger generation step up and play a bigger role in the reunions.

PEACHES. That's right. And since Uncle Aubrey's ninetieth birthday's coming up, Gaynelle's gonna … make him a cake. *(Pointedly.)* Right, Gaynelle?

GAYNELLE. *(Trapped.)* Right. I'm gonna make him a … um … red velvet cake.

LA MERLE. Is that so? Then you tell me how in the world you think you're gonna pull this off.

GAYNELLE. *(Scrambles.)* Well, you see … I mean … Uh, well, I have —

LA MERLE. *(Leans on the table.)* What you *have* is no earthly idea of the mess you're about to make. *(Lifts her sticky hand.)* You know, if you'd spend less time publicizing your failures and more time keeping house, you'd be better off! Disgusting! *(Exits to the kitchen.)*

PEACHES. That holier-than-thou harpy has bossed and bullied everybody in this family for as long as we can remember, but we can't let her do it this time. You *have* to host the reunion.

JIMMIE WYVETTE. To be fair, LaMerle *did* teach me two real important things, one is that sex is the most awful, filthy thing on earth and I should save it for someone I love. The other is that God loves me and I'm gonna burn in hell.

PEACHES. Two *more* reasons that woman's gotta be put in her place. The stakes are too high! *(To Gaynelle.)* Come on girl, you've got to find your strength!

GAYNELLE. I know you mean well, but I've got nothing left. LaMerle is so mean and I am so tired, I just can't do — *(LaMerle enters from the kitchen.)*

LA MERLE. Well, now we know where the ebola virus was hatched. Right out there in that sink. And the thought of the family choking down something you made in that nasty kitchen is nothing but inhumane. So, I've made your decision. This year's reunion is off.

GAYNELLE. Well, now, let's not be too hasty … I mean, there's still time to … uh, I'm pretty sure the three of us might be able to manage to hold the family —

LA MERLE. I've thought it over and I'm right. You could no more get a reunion organized in this filthy house than you could hang onto your husband.

GAYNELLE. *(A flame flickers.)* Excuse me? What did you just say?

JIMMIE WYVETTE. Aunt LaMerle, that topic's not open for discussion.

PEACHES. *(Low, to Jimmie Wyvette.)* Hang on! This may be exactly what we need to get Gaynelle back in the game!

GAYNELLE. Let me make this clear, Aunt LaMerle. You are not welcome to discuss the events of my personal life, unhappy or otherwise, with me or anyone else. *(Pushes up her sleeves.)*

JIMMIE WYVETTE. *(Low, to Peaches.)* Uh-oh. She's pushing up the sleeves. This is gonna be good.

GAYNELLE. After all the emotional abuse I've taken from my former husband, his girlfriend, his lawyer and various knuckle-dragging officers of the law, I'll be damned if I take any from *family.*

PEACHES. *(Low, to Jimmie Wyvette.)* I've waited twenty-five years for this. Let's get a good seat. *(They hurry to the couch, sit. Gaynelle and LaMerle square off on opposite ends of the couch.)*

LA MERLE. *(Incensed.)* How dare you!

GAYNELLE. *(Rants.)* I'll tell you exactly *how,* Miss Sour Britches!

JIMMIE WYVETTE. *(Low, to Peaches.)* Ooh! She'll pay for that one.

GAYNELLE. *(Confidence gradually increases.)* Oh, I'm hosting this reunion, alright, and it's gonna be the best one in Verdeen family history. And it'll be a really good time *for a change,* unlike the constipated snooze-fests you throw every year. And you know what? I'll bake Uncle Aubrey the most incredible red velvet cake he's ever laid tongue to! And you'll just have to shut your yap and accept it.

PEACHES. *(Low.)* Okay, shug, you've found your strength. That's enough.

LA MERLE. *(Fumes.)* Is that so? Well, let me tell you something: You couldn't beat my red velvet cake if you spent the rest of your life trying.

GAYNELLE. Wanna bet?

PEACHES. Uh ... Gaynelle, darlin' —

LA MERLE. Why, yes, ma'am. I'd be proud to make you a bet.

JIMMIE WYVETTE. Gaynelle, you better stop while you're —

GAYNELLE. *(Drunk on confidence.)* You are on! Whip up that red velvet mess you're so proud of. We'll set 'em side by side and just see who makes the best cake. Ooh! Tell you what, when I *win,* I get

21

Grandmary's quilt. You know, the one she gave *me*, but that some-how wound up in *your* front bedroom the day of her funeral *where it's been ever since!*

LA MERLE. A piddling old quilt? That's it? Well, for someone like you, I guess that's a pretty important prize. But you can forget it, missy, since you've got nothing left from your disastrous divorce to offer when *I* win. *(Starts for the door.)*

GAYNELLE. Hold on! I've got ... well, for one thing there's my — *(Glances desperately around the room for an asset.)*

JIMMIE WYVETTE. Face it, Gaynelle. You've got nothing left worth diddly except this house.

GAYNELLE. That's it!

PEACHES. Gaynelle, no! Don't —

GAYNELLE. I'm so sure my cake will win, I'll bet my *house* on it.

JIMMIE WYVETTE. No, Gaynelle! Aunt LaMerle, she doesn't mean —

LA MERLE. It's a deal! *(They shake.)* You girls are my witnesses. Handshake's the same as a contract. And you may be right about one thing, Gaynelle, this could turn out to be the best family reunion yet. *(Exits.)*

JIMMIE WYVETTE. *(Horrified.)* Woman, what have you just done?!

PEACHES. Shug, you do realize there are people who would crawl through burning mesquite chips for just one bite of LaMerle's red velvet cake, don't you?

GAYNELLE. *(Exultant.)* Oh, I'm too happy to worry about that now! I just put LaMerle in her place at long last! This is going to be great! *(Marches resolutely to the kitchen door. Turns back.)* Oh, I do have a question, though. Anybody know how to make a red velvet cake? *(She exits into the kitchen. Stunned, Peaches and Jimmie Wyvette stare after her. Peaches takes a hit of whipped cream. Jimmie Wyvette opens her mouth, Peaches gives her a hit, too. Blackout.)*

Scene 6

The next evening. Lights up center stage on Gaynelle's living room. Peaches paces nervously as she makes notes on a clipboard. Jimmie Wyvette races in the front door with her clipboard.

JIMMIE WYVETTE. I finished my list!

PEACHES. So did I! Now, I realize we're probably running on pure adrenaline 'cause we're only a day away from the reunion, but I'm feeling pretty good about what we've actually accomplished so far.

JIMMIE WYVETTE. Me, too. We're set with the community room, they're getting some extra tables and chairs in from Wynette's Dinette City. There'll be dominoes for the forty-two competition and Audra Crump's bringing her hymn-singing birds and hinted they might be talked into performing "How Great Thou Art." Fingers crossed!

PEACHES. Talk about fine entertainment! Course, we'll have to kiss our cleaning deposit goodbye.

JIMMIE WYVETTE. So, what about the pot-luck?

PEACHES. Well, my news isn't quite as splashy. Every Verdeen who's coming insists on bringing beans: baked beans, butter beans, pinto beans, three-bean salad — oh, and for a change of pace, Ninah Lee's bringing wieners and beans.

JIMMIE WYVETTE. Great. Like this family needs to tank up on *beans.*

PEACHES. Rusty over at Pawnee's Quik 'Que is smoking us a ten-pound ham and deep-frying a turkey. So right now it's looking like meat and beans with a side of meat and beans. Which reminds me, I ran into Zelma Hackett who said she'd whipped up a batch of Venison Helper for Burton Pearsol. The race is on, Jimmie Wy.

JIMMIE WYVETTE. I did like you said. I made prune roll-ups and took 'em over this morning. But when I got there, Bitsy was prancing in his back door with a coffee cake and locked me out. Lucky for me, I was able to break in through the laundry room window or it would've been a monstrous waste of time. Bitsy was some kind of surprised when I waltzed into that kitchen and handed Burton my roll-ups. You said stake out my territory, and stake it out, I did! *(Gaynelle, frazzled, wearing a white apron splotched with large red stains, exits the kitchen.)*

GAYNELLE. Listen, where do y'all suppose I could — *(Peaches and Jimmie Wyvette simultaneously shriek at the sight of what appears to be her "bloody" apron.)*

JIMMIE WYVETTE. My God, Gaynelle, you did it! You finally killed Sumner!

PEACHES. Oh, darlin' girl, we cannot get you out of *this* one!

JIMMIE WYVETTE. Wait! I have an idea! We soak Sumner's body in a tub of syrup, wrap it in sheets with a bungee cord, haul it out to the woods, wedge it in the fork of a tree and let wild animals devour it. What do you think? *(Peaches and Gaynelle stare at her, dumbfounded.)*

PEACHES. I think that psychologist is coming to evaluate the wrong Verdeen! Now Gaynelle, take off that bloody apron! We've got to get rid of the evidence.

GAYNELLE. Take off the wha — ? *(It dawns on her.)* For heaven's sake, it's food coloring! I haven't resorted to murder *yet.*

JIMMIE WYVETTE. Oh. Well, that's a shame, 'cause I'm positive my soakin'-the-body-in-syrup idea would've worked like gangbusters.

GAYNELLE. Listen, I don't have *time* to kill Sumner. I've been through all my cookbooks, made a dozen different cakes and every one I've baked is either too dry, too gooey or too vinegary. Lucky number thirteen's in the oven and now I've run out of red food coloring! I called Tootie Rose at the mini-mart and she told me LaMerle was in this morning and bought her last six bottles. She's trying to make sure I can't find any. Girls, this means *war!*

JIMMIE WYVETTE. Oh, this is *classic* La Merle.

PEACHES. I knew she'd play dirty! Gaynelle, you keep looking for a recipe and we'll find — Oops! My beeper. *(Checks it.)* Oh, just a test. With this heat wave, my mortuaries have me on high alert. These Yankee transplants tend to drop like flies when we hit triple digits. I better go juice up my cell. *(Exits the front door.)*

GAYNELLE. *(Calls after her.)* I'm borrowing your emery board! My nails feel like I worked 'em over with a cheese grater.

JIMMIE WYVETTE. I keep my nails neat by gnawing 'em down even. Want me to give yours a shot?

GAYNELLE. Uh … I'll pass. *(Opens Peaches' bag.)* Here's that envelope again. Wonder what's in here Peaches wanted to discuss?

JIMMIE WYVETTE. *(Snatches it away.)* Stop that! You know it's wrong to go snooping through someone's private papers.

GAYNELLE. *(Snatches it back.)* I beg to differ. For example, you might find motel bills for romantic getaways *you* never knew about or signs your life savings were siphoned away *before* your marriage-made-in-heaven turned into the ninth circle of hell!

JIMMIE WYVETTE. *(Beat.)* Well, what're you waiting for? *(Gaynelle takes out a document, they read.)* No! She can't be serious about this!

GAYNELLE. *(Puts the document back.)* She's coming. Okay, we didn't see a thing. We don't say a word.

JIMMIE WYVETTE. Right. You can count on me.

PEACHES. Lor-dee! It is hotter than —

JIMMIE WYVETTE. *(Blurts out.)* Gaynelle went through your things and read your private papers! I watched her do it!

GAYNELLE. *(To Jimmie Wyvette.)* I can count on you to *what*, hurl me off a bridge?! *(To Peaches.)* Okay, I'm sorry.

PEACHES. Don't be! I'm so relieved you did. I've wanted to talk to y'all about this for months. I'm torn about whether or not to go through with it.

JIMMIE WYVETTE. Portia Louise Verdeen Belrose, you cannot declare your husband dead! There's no body, so you can't prove T. Rex is gone.

GAYNELLE. I'm with Jimmie Wy. I mean, if you're not sure, maybe you better give it some more time. 'Cause once you sign those papers, it cannot be undone.

PEACHES. The man's been missing for seven long years! I sold the house to pay his debts, I built up my business, worked like a dog, all the time wondering what on earth I did to deserve this. Girls, waiting in an RV for a *no-show* every night is no kind of life and I am *done!* Besides, I've been feeling certain ... *urges* lately.

JIMMIE WYVETTE. What kind of urges?

PEACHES. You know, *urges.* It's been ages since I've been with a man and I have ... *needs.*

JIMMIE WYVETTE. What kind of needs?

PEACHES. *(Explodes.)* The concept is not that hard to grasp! Look, when I was young and single, I know there were some people who might've called me wild —

JIMMIE WYVETTE. Or "tramp." Or "Peaches, the Mattress." Or —

PEACHES. *My point is* when Rex and I *did* get together we were a darn good match. It was a very *satisfying* marriage in many ways. So, when you don't have that warm body next to you every night, things feel out of whack. I just can't stand it anymore! Girls, the truth of it is, these luscious lips were meant to be kissed!

GAYNELLE. Uh, Peaches, do you really think you ought to tell us —

PEACHES. *(With increasing fervor.)* These curves were meant to be caressed —

JIMMIE WYVETTE. Maybe we should change the subject —

PEACHES. This trembling body was meant to be —

GAYNELLE. Peaches! Gee! We get it, okay?! Don't paint pictures we can't scrub off the walls of our memory!

JIMMIE WYVETTE. *(Sniffs the air.)* Hold on! Y'all smell that? Reckon Mama Doll's trying to deep fry Bitsy's sock monkey again?

GAYNELLE. Oh, no! Cake number thirteen! *(Races to the kitchen door. Exits.)*

JIMMIE WYVETTE. *(Shakes her head.)* Another *dead* velvet cake. Look, Peaches, we're with you, no matter what you decide about T. Rex. Hey, this is the first time in years the three of us have had men on the brain at the same time. I'm trying to snare one, you're trying to bury one and Gaynelle wants to kill one.

PEACHES. Historically, Verdeen women haven't exactly had the greatest success with the opposite sex. We ought to just hang out a sign that says, "Decent guys wanted. No weirdos need apply." *(Doorbell rings. She opens the door. Newt Blaylock, a high-energy, true Texas eccentric with a patch over one eye, holds a foam head wearing a platinum blonde beehive wig.)*

JIMMIE WYVETTE. *(Low, to Peaches.)* We waited too long to hang that sign.

NEWT. Hey, ladies! Look who's *hair!* *(Laughs at his own joke.)*

PEACHES. *(Suddenly flirtatious.)* Well, hell-o! That was one fast delivery! Thanks for driving all the way over from Tenaha.

NEWT. Yes, ma'am, Newt Blaylock at your service. We aim to please at Miss Treeva's Wig 'N' Bait!

PEACHES. It's just unbelievable we've only spoken on the phone. *(Seductively.)* If I'd known what I was missing, I might've driven over earlier and checked out your ... nightcrawlers. *(Jimmie Wyvette gives her a disapproving look.)*

NEWT. *(Gives her the wig.)* Here you go. The Gospel Jubilee

Beehive, Number 603, just like you ordered. Let me tell you, it wasn't easy to find.

PEACHES. Well, I got a heads up from Flawney Jernigan in the ER that Nettioma Bartay is barely hanging on. And her last wish is to hit those pearly gates sportin' the same 'do she had on her weddin' day. So, I wanted to locate one now in case Nettioma passes during our family reunion. Oh, excuse me. I don't believe you know my cousin, Jimmie Wyvette! *(Low, to Jimmie Wyvette.)* Don't mention his eye!

JIMMIE WYVETTE. *(Whispers.)* 'Course not! Trust me. *(To Newt, they shake.)* Actually, we met at the store. Not every day a one-eyed man walks into Whatley's.

PEACHES. *(Elbows her, then, quickly:)* So, Newt, I know Miss Treeva passed. Is it hard running the Wig 'N' Bait by yourself?

NEWT. Well, I miss Mama something terrible — she had a true feel for crickets and bloodworms — but I'm okay. I'm a champ at adjusting. I learned early on.

JIMMIE WYVETTE. 'Cause of the one eye and all? *(Peaches elbows her.)*

NEWT. That *was* a big part of it. See, I married right out of high school. Maryjack MacLemore was head twirler senior year and I tell you, her fire baton routine to the theme from *Bonanza* got me where I lived. We moved in with Mama who never allowed twirling in the house and I made the tragic mistake of giving Maryjack a new baton that first Christmas. She was so happy, she threw the baton toward the ceiling, it knocked off the pointy tree topper, which came at my face like a projectile missile and ... need I say more? Yeah, the marriage was pretty much over after that. Maryjack moved to Fayro to teach twirling and dance. But that event taught me I could adjust to anything. Yes, ma'am, I'm stronger for it. I am a *rock*.

PEACHES. *(Reaches for his bicep.)* Why, I just bet you are. *(Before she can touch him, Jimmie Wyvette quickly slaps Peaches' hand away as Gaynelle enters from the kitchen with a slice of cake, a can of whipped cream in her apron pocket.)*

GAYNELLE. Well, the cake's not burned. I pulled it out at the last minute.

NEWT. Wow! It's *you!* *(Pushes past Peaches.)* I am spitting distance from an actual TV star! I saw you yesterday on *Hospitality House!* And, hand to God, your butt's not half as big as the camera made

27

it look!

JIMMIE WYVETTE. Gaynelle, meet Newt Blaylock, *the rock.*

NEWT. *(Gushes.)* 'Scuse me for carrying on, but I was knocked out by your performance. It was so … *pathetic!* I mean, I've never seen anyone who needed a hug as bad as you! *(Grabs her in an awkward hug. Gaynelle's bewildered. Then.)* There. Now, can I do anything for you? Anything at all?

GAYNELLE. Well, uh … I do need some red food coloring.

NEWT. Red food coloring? I'm on it! *(Races out the front door. Peaches crosses to the front door, yells after him.)*

PEACHES. And while you're away, I'll be thinking of a few things you and those muscles of yours can do for *me!*

JIMMIE WYVETTE. *(To Peaches.)* You *do* remember you're still married, right?

PEACHES. *(Pulls the document from her purse.)* Not anymore! *(Signs it.)* I did it! I am now officially the Widow Belrose! I'm free! *(Laughs maniacally.)*

GAYNELLE. Uh-oh. We got us a widow with urges *and* an RV.

JIMMIE WYVETTE. There's not an unmarried man in Texas who's safe now.

PEACHES. Oh, girls, I know I did the right thing! There's a brand-new beautiful life waiting for me! Gaynelle, mind if I go after Mr. Sexy Eyepatch?

GAYNELLE. Frankly, it would be a relief!

PEACHES. Perfect! Let's celebrate! *(Takes the cake. She and Jimmie Wyvette sample a bite.)*

GAYNELLE. I think I finally got it right. This is *the one.* So, is it good? *(They make approving sounds.)* Is it great?! *(More approving sounds.)* Better than LaMerle's?

JIMMIE WYVETTE. Not even close. *(Peaches agrees.)*

GAYNELLE. I'm doomed! *(Takes the can of cream out of her pocket, squirts some into her mouth.)*

PEACHES. *(Snatches the can away.)* I'm so sorry, shug, but you picked the wrong battle with LaMerle.

GAYNELLE. I just lost my head, okay? But she gets my goat! Every time I see her I think about the quilt she stole and I want it back! When we were little and Grandmary tucked it around the three of us, it felt like nothing bad could ever happen.

PEACHES. Remember how we'd make a tent with that quilt, get under it and drink cocoa when it rained? I can't remember being that kind of happy since.

JIMMIE WYVETTE. It was our security blanket. That quilt made everything right. *(They sigh. Then, blunt.)* Too bad you're going to lose your house over it.

PEACHES. She is *not* going to lose this house! Gaynelle, you march right over there, call LaMerle and tell her you didn't mean it, you were high on Maalox, *anything.* Surely she'll have the decency not to hold you to that bet. *(LaMerle barrels through the front door with a tape measure.)*

LA MERLE. *(Sings.)* ONWARD CHRISTIAN SOLDIERS, MARCHING AS TO WAR. WITH THE CROSS OF —*(Quickly measures a wall.)* Perfect! A couch will fit right here. *(Then, to Gaynelle.)* Guess there's no point in asking how your cake's coming along! *(Roars with laughter as she exits. Beat.)*

JIMMIE WYVETTE. Come on, y'all, *think!* We're out of time. The reunion's tomorrow! We need a great recipe *now!*

PEACHES. Well, Grandmary always said Belva Clay Stansil's cake was so good, governors would ask her to ship 'em one to Austin now and then.

GAYNELLE. Yeah, but selfish old Belva Clay vowed she'd take the recipe with her to the grave so nobody else could have it. And she did.

JIMMIE WYVETTE. Wait! I remember a story about the mayor guilt-tripping Belva Clay into donating a copy of her recipe for the town's time capsule.

PEACHES. Even if he did, what good does that do us? The thing's been buried almost thirty years now. Like we're going to go behind the courthouse and *dig it up? (Beat. She and Gaynelle slowly turn to Jimmie Wyvette. That's exactly what's on Jimmie Wyvette's mind. Then.)* Oh, no you don't! No way, no how!

JIMMIE WYVETTE. Nobody has to know! We just dig it up, copy the recipe, and put it back in the ground. Easy.

GAYNELLE. *(Angry.)* Do I need to remind you that I have only recently avoided incarceration? And now you want me to risk being arrested *again* just to make a cake that's going to save my house and rub LaMerle's nose in it?! *(Long beat.)* Okay, I'll get the shovel.

PEACHES. I'll get the axe.

JIMMIE WYVETTE. And I'll get the rope. We leave at midnight!

GAYNELLE. And if I do wind up behind bars, at least I won't be alone.

PEACHES. Yeah, 'cause cousins are kinda like brassieres. They're always close to your heart and when you start to sag, they'll be there to support you. *(They laugh. Blackout.)*

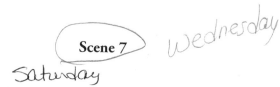

Scene 7 *Wednesday*

Saturday

Early the next morning. Lights up center stage on Gaynelle's living room. Someone covered with a blanket sleeps on the couch and the beehive wig sits on the dining table. There's a knock at the door. Newt opens the door and peeks in.

NEWT. *(Calls.)* Anybody home? *(Beat. Enters with a bouquet of flowers.)* Hello? *(The sleeping person moves and makes a muffled noise. Newt crosses to the couch.)* I know it's early, Gaynelle, but I couldn't sleep and I had to bring you these to apologize for the way I acted yesterday. I had a powerful reaction to you, the likes of which I've only felt once before, with my ex. *(No response. Sits on the armchair beside the couch.)* I know you're having a hard time right now and I don't want to be another rough patch in your already miserable life. *(Turns away, shy.)* But it's hard not to be attracted to you. *(Unnoticed, Uncle Aubrey throws off the blanket, sits up, studies Newt.)* Your skin's so pale and soft-lookin', you've got two of the most expressive eyes and believe me, I pay attention to *that* kind of thing. Anyway, I hope when you look at these flowers you'll think of me and how sorry I am.

AUBREY. Son, it'll take a damn sight more than flowers to win *my* affection. *(Cackles. Startled, Newt lurches around and knocks himself off the chair.)*

NEWT. *(With a yelp!)* What the — ? What're *you* doing here?!

AUBREY. Listening to a man who doesn't know the first thing about women.

NEWT. Hey, I know stuff! It's not like I need advice or — *(Then.)* Oh, who am I fooling? I sell wigs and worms for a living, and the only woman I've taken out to supper in the last two decades was *my mama!* Who's gonna want to date *me?*

30

AUBREY. Hold on! You don't look so sorry to me. No, sir, you're not in half-bad shape. Iron your shirt, shine your shoes, buy a new eye, you'll be good to go.

NEWT. I'm not so sure. Truth is, Gaynelle's way out of my league.

AUBREY. Horse manukey! Go for it, son! You've got to live each day as if it's your last, 'cause one day you'll be *right!* (Cackles.) Now, I didn't get to be two hundred years old without learning a few things about the ladies, so ditch the flowers and give Gaynelle what she *really* wants. (Pulls a bottle out of his pocket.)

NEWT. Red food coloring! Dang! I looked all over McTwayne County for some of this.

AUBREY. I bet you did. See, I smelled a rat when my scheming niece, LaMerle, showed up with a car full of these little bottles. She let it slip she and Gaynelle have a bakin' battle brewin', so I swiped one for Gaynelle and you're giving it to her.

NEWT. Well, thanks! How can I return the favor?

AUBREY. Hand over them flowers and walk me next door. I've got a hot date with my honey.

NEWT. (Takes the food coloring, helps Aubrey to the front door.) A girlfriend at your age? You really *do* know your stuff!

AUBREY. Gaynelle lets me cat-nap on her couch to get my mojo perking. Yeah, Mama Doll's worth it, but we have to do our cuddlin' early because by ten A.M., my energy's shot and Mama Doll's forgotten who I am. Hey, you know the nice thing about dating a gal with short-term memory loss? The romance is always new! (Cackles as Newt helps him out the front door. Beat. Peaches, dressed in black with a black wool cap and a pair of sunglasses, sticks her head in the kitchen door and looks around.)

PEACHES. Okay, the coast is clear. (Peeks out as Gaynelle and Jimmie Wyvette, dressed similarly, struggle in through the kitchen door with a large, heavy object, draped in a dirt-smeared tarp.) Get a move on! Stop dragging your feet!

GAYNELLE. What's in this capsule, anyway? Cannonballs from the Battle of San Jacinto?

JIMMIE WYVETTE. I'm getting a cramp! We've got to set it down! (They quick-step toward the dining table.)

PEACHES. Not there! You'll ruin the finish!

JIMMIE WYVETTE. (Hustles toward the buffet.) Over here! Hurry!

PEACHES. No! It's too high!

JIMMIE WYVETTE. It's slipping! We're gonna crash!

PEACHES. Coffee table! Get it to the coffee table!

GAYNELLE. *(Frantic.)* It's too flimsy!

JIMMIE WYVETTE. It's going! It's going! *(Amid Gaynelle and Peaches' screams, they scurry to the couch, heave the object up onto the cushions. Jimmie Wyvette and Gaynelle collapse, exhausted.)*

PEACHES. *(Drops into the armchair.)* Well, that like to have killed me. *(Gaynelle and Jimmie Wyvette share a look. Gaynelle hurls a throw pillow at Peaches.)* Hey! Is it *my* fault you two are so out of shape?

GAYNELLE. Don't start up on that. I want nothing to do with exercise. I tried yoga once and hated it. I spent an hour pushing, pulling, stretching, straining. By the time I finally got into those tights, the class was over.

JIMMIE WYVETTE. After hoisting off the two-ton plaque that marked the spot so we could dig the five feet to get to *this* lead weight, I've had all the exercise *I'm* gonna need for the rest of my life.

PEACHES. Look, let's just open the time capsule, copy that recipe and thank our lucky stars that nobody knows what we're up to. *(They start to remove the tarp, Bitsy barges in the front door with an empty dish. Gaynelle immediately drapes herself awkwardly across the top of the capsule to "hide" it.)*

BITSY. Knockety-knock-knock! I was just — Oh, look how you're dressed! Guess this will teach y'all to call each other in the morning before you leave the house.

GAYNELLE. What a great tip! Thanks so much. Now, don't let us hold you up!

BITSY. Oh, you're not. I just scooted over to give Aubrey and Mama Doll a little "alone time" while they have their morning snack. They are *so* cute to watch … until they start feeding each other puddin'. *(Shudders.)*

JIMMIE WYVETTE. *(Suspicious.)* So, Bitsy, what're you doing with my Pyrex?

BITSY. See, after you left Burton's yesterday, I started cleaning his kitchen. He loves the way I tidy up. I'd turned away just a second and his Great Dane licked your plate clean. Thinking back, I guess I shouldn't have put your Pyrex on the floor. *(Hands Jimmie Wyvette the dish.)*

JIMMIE WYVETTE. *(Stunned.)* Trinket ate my roll-ups?!

BITSY. You really don't need to bother bringing anything else over.

Burton's taken a real shine to my cooking and I've got everything under control. *(Pointedly.)* And I intend to keep it that way. Bye-dee-bye-bye! *(Exits the front door.)*

JIMMIE WYVETTE. That does it! I'm gonna feed *her* to the dog! *(Jimmie Wyvette lunges for the door. Peaches and Gaynelle hold her back.)*

GAYNELLE. Stop it! You've already broken six or eight laws this morning. Don't make it worse by killing a priss-pot before noon!

PEACHES. Forget that! Let's just get this time capsule open while nobody's here but us. *(Newt bursts through the front door. Jimmie Wyvette throws herself on top of the time capsule and feigns a relaxed pose.)*

NEWT. 'Scuse me! But I saw you pull in and I wanted to give you —

GAYNELLE. Actually, we're a little busy, Newt. Maybe you could come back another —

PEACHES. *(Smitten, plants herself between Newt and Gaynelle.)* Unless there's anything *I* can do for you. *(Suggestively.)* *Anything* at all.

NEWT. *(Shifts from side to side to try to see around Peaches. She mirrors his movements.)* Actually, Gaynelle, it's more like *me* doing something for *you*. I am — I have — 'Scuse me. *(Moves Peaches aside. Pulls the small bottle from his pocket.)* Red food coloring. Just like you wanted!

GAYNELLE. Wow, you actually found some! Thank you, Newt. If you come across any more in the next few hours, keep us in mind.

NEWT. You need more? I'm on it! *(Sprints out the front door. Jimmie Wyvette gets a screwdriver and works on the capsule during the following.)*

PEACHES. *(Calls after him.)* Hurry right back! I'll be counting the minutes while you're gone. *(Makes kissing noises and waves after him.)*

GAYNELLE. Will you give it a rest, Miss Sizzle Britches?! We don't have time for that now. Or ever, really. We've got to get this thing open, bake the cake and clean this house for the reunion, get ready for the psychologist and —

JIMMIE WYVETTE. You two stop squawking and get over here! I'm in! *(Gaynelle and Peaches hurry over.)*

PEACHES. Oh, my gosh! We're about to open the Sweetgum time capsule! This must be how it felt when they discovered King Tut's tomb.

JIMMIE WYVETTE. Oh, it's even better. Aren't you excited?

GAYNELLE. I will be when we have Belva Clay's recipe in our hands! Here we go! One-two-three! *(They lift off the heavy top.*

Joyous squeals, then silence. Scoops up a sticky, soggy mess.) Reckon this used to be the recipe?

JIMMIE WYVETTE. Pee-yew! What moron didn't think to waterproof this thing?

GAYNELLE. Everything's ruined! When they open this in seventy years they'll think we were dumber than an armadillo handbag.

PEACHES. And yet, *(Pulls out a foil-wrapped brick of Velveeta.)* this Velveeta is as nice and fresh as it was the day it came off the grocery shelf.

JIMMIE WYVETTE. Can you beat that! Gaynelle, got any crackers? *(Unnoticed, Sheriff Grover Lout, with mirrored shades and a bad attitude, eases in through the kitchen door. Both hands on his pistol, he aims at the trio.)*

GAYNELLE. The recipe's ruined?! Then, it's over! LaMerle gets my house, Sumner gets the redhead and I get the funny farm! My life is over! *(Screams.)* AHHHH! *(Taken by surprise, Sheriff Lout drops to the floor.)*

PEACHES. *(Sweetly.)* Aw, Gaynelle, it'll be alright somehow. Don't give up.

GROVER. *(Springs to his feet, gun aimed.)* No, *all* of you give up! *(The trio screams in unison. Startled, Grover flings his gun over his shoulder, scrambles to retrieve it and covers.)* Freeze! *(They do.)* That's better! Well, this is one for the books! Catching an entire gang of county property desecrators. To celebrate, I brought y'all a little gift. *(Takes out two pair of handcuffs.)* Look! Jewelry! *(Handcuffs them together.)*

GAYNELLE. I can't go to jail, I've got to bake a cake!

PEACHES. And I've got to find a man!

JIMMIE WYVETTE. And I've got to kill the neighbor! *(Off Grover's look, covers.)* With … kindness. She's a great gal.

GROVER. Didn't take much to follow your trail, Peaches, since you made your getaway in that souped-up RV of yours. I'm arresting y'all for criminal trespass, theft, larceny and whatever else I can come up with when I get back to the office and look through the manual.

JIMMIE WYVETTE. Don't take this as a threat, Grover, but this pretty much puts the kay-bosh on your twenty-percent belt and boot discount down at Whatley's.

GAYNELLE. This isn't happening! Can my life get any worse? *(Elsa Dowdall, European-born, stern and ultra-efficient, bursts through the front door.)*

ELSA. I'm Elsa Dowdall, court-appointed psychologist. Veech of you ees Gaynelle Verdeen Bodeen? *(Gaynelle immediately faints in Peaches' arms. Grover herds the cousins toward the door. Peaches drags Gaynelle's limp body.)*

PEACHES. Make yourself at home, Elsa. Tea's in the fridge!

JIMMIE WYVETTE. Just so you know, us Verdeens are a pretty dull bunch. Just your average, normal family. No nut jobs here. *(Grover yanks them out the front door. Immediately, Uncle Aubrey, his face covered in lipstick kisses, wheels in his oxygen tank and shuffles as fast as he can from the kitchen. Mama Doll, in a lacy little old lady dress and cowboy boots, shuffles after him in hot pursuit.)*

MAMA DOLL. Wait 'til I get my hands on you, you hunk-a hunk-a burnin' love!

AUBREY. Last one to the hot tub buys the tequila! *(Elsa watches with dismay as they round the couch, stop to catch their breath, then resume the race out the kitchen door. Blackout.)*

End of Act One

ACT TWO

Wednesday [handwritten]

Scene 1

~~Saturday~~ [handwritten]

Later that morning. Lights up center stage on the Hospitality House *"set." Cee Cee wears a frilly apron and addresses "the camera."*

CEE CEE. Thanks for joining me again this morning here on *Hospitality House*, where we check our firearms at the door and enjoy a half hour of gracious living. Now, in our Saturday diet segment, Skinny Fixin's, Velour Parmer from Parmer's Pork Palace is going to show us a nifty new way to de-fat a butt roast. Then later I'll be whipping up an Aegean holiday feast, Greek dishes that are impossible to pronounce, but delicious to eat. But first, let's go to our viewer mail. *(Picks up a letter.)* Leota Troutner over in Bobo writes: "Cee Cee, my husband makes terrible grease stains on my dining table when he works on his carburetor. How can I get them off and make sure there's no permanent damage to my wood-like veneer?" Excellent question, Leota. Here's what you do: First remove the carburetor from the table, wipe up the grease with a soft cloth moistened with mineral oil and buff it to a shine. Then when your husband goes to work, call Blue down at the hardware store, have him change all the locks on your doors and *file for divorce.* Trust me, girlfriend, this little household tip will protect the finish on that dining table *for life! Now,* I'll be right back after this message, so why don't you come on back, too? *(Drops her on-camera persona, frantically motions offstage.)* Hurry! I only have ninety seconds! *(Gaynelle, in a sweatsuit, her hair in a roller cap, staggers on with two heavy shopping bags.)*

GAYNELLE. I took everything out of the freezer back there. You're sure you don't mind me taking all this Indian food?

CEE CEE. Please, that whole show, *Bombay Buffet,* was a dud. I honestly believe Texans are genetically pre-disposed to fear tandoori. My crew wouldn't touch it with a ten-foot pole. Hope you have better luck with the Verdeens.

GAYNELLE. Sorry I called you so early, but when Grover finally let us go, we realized we wouldn't have time to cook. And the reunion's this afternoon.

CEE CEE. *I'm* sorry I was out of town and couldn't help you with your cake so this mess could've been avoided. But why did Grover release you without pressing charges?

GAYNELLE. Peaches saw him eyein' her RV and told him, given enough motivation, she might be willing to sell it to him at a deep discount. So, he took the bait and we got off the hook!

CEE CEE. Makes me proud to know we live in a place where you can still bribe your way out of a legal jam. So, are you all set? What about the cake?

GAYNELLE. We thought we were sunk when we saw Belva Clay's recipe had disintegrated, but when Grover took us to jail, there was a framed picture of her presenting the recipe to the mayor hangin' on the wall. So, I stole *that* when Grover wasn't looking!

CEE CEE. Girl, this crime wave has got to stop, you hear? *(Concerned.)* But Belva Clay's recipe? Are you *sure?*

GAYNELLE. Yeah, now all I've got to do is get a magnifying glass to read the recipe so I can bake the cake that'll save my home then redeem myself with the psychologist by throwing a whiz-bang reunion that'll keep me off the funny farm. *(Notices "the camera.")* That flashing light means something, right? *(Exits.)*

CEE CEE. Harley, I swore if you did this to me again, I'd kick your — *(Turns to "the camera," all smiles.)* As I was saying, today's show is jam-packed and fun-filled, so hang onto your housecoat because — *(Gaynelle hustles across the stage, trying to find the exit. Cee Cee watches. Then.)* … because I'm thinking we're in for one ring-tailed-tooter of a Saturday here in Sweetgum! *(Blackout.)*

Scene 2

One hour later. Lights up center stage on Gaynelle's living room. Peaches, in a bathrobe, quickly cleans up. Elsa sits nearby. The beehive wig is on the table.

ELSA. Yes, I haf verked as a psychologist in zis country many years vith my late husband, Wictor. After he vas discharged from zee Army, he told me there vas a vast need for mental health professionals in zis state und, oh boy, vas he right. I understand zee Texas mind as Wictor and his pipple vere all from Vichita Falls. Mercifully, I do not have to deal vith them anymore because they are all now dead.

PEACHES. Yeah, we're looking forward to that happy day with a few of our relatives, too.

ELSA. Vell, good luck vith that. Now, let us review vhat happened earlier.

PEACHES. The whole thing came about because of Gaynelle's dedication to volunteerism. She found out Sheriff Lout needed help with his *training exercise*, and bam! She signed us up and we *pretended* to break the law so he could practice arresting people. That's Gaynelle: civic booster clear down to her shorts.

ELSA. *(Fans.)* Vell, I hope zis *unusual* statement ees correct, because nutting vill blind me from zee truth, not even in zis blazing heat. I must decide for zee court eef your cousin ees a menace to society and should be sent avay. Should I discover your statement is less than —

PEACHES. True?! Of course it is! Listen, only a *nut* would actually steal a time capsule from a courthouse lawn! Not Gaynelle. She's the sanest woman alive!

GAYNELLE. *(Bursts through the kitchen door, unaware of Elsa's presence. Frazzled, still in the roller cap, a can of whipped cream in her pocket.)* Well, the dad-blamed cake's in the oven! If Belva Clay hadn't already croaked, I'd strangle that old biddy for making her recipe so hard. *(Peaches tries to interrupt.)* Oh, yeah, Aunt LaMerle called, heard you're officially a widow and said you'd better act like one in public *or else.* So, please wear something black today just to *shut her up!* And for the last time, will you get that dead woman's hair off my table before I take a chainsaw to it?! *(Pulls out the can of cream, takes a hit.)*

PEACHES. *(Grabs the can. Then, sweet but pointedly.)* Gaynelle, darlin', I was just telling Ms. Dowdall here about our little *exercise* last night and your spirit of volunteerism.

GAYNELLE. *(Catches on.)* Oh! Right … right! That's me. Give, give, give! Matter of fact … *(Fans Elsa vigoriously.)* let me *give* you a little relief from this heat. Of course my A.C. *would* have to conk out on the hottest day in July.

ELSA. *(Jots in her notebook.)* So, tell me, Gaynelle, do you find your temper flares in zee heat? Maybe you vant to go after someone vith, maybe, a machete?

PEACHES. Of course not! Gaynelle's very even-tempered. Watch, she won't even flinch when I tell her they've double-booked the community room with the Petal Pushers Garden Show so we're going to have to have the reunion *right here.*

GAYNELLE. What?! *(Newt enters the front door with a hammer and a saw.)*

NEWT. I have no idea how to fix your A.C., Gaynelle. Fact is, I may have made it worse, 'cause now I think it's stuck on *heat.*

GAYNELLE. *(Explodes.)* The entire Verdeen clan will be here in less than two hours and now *this?!* Only a lame-brained dodo would — *(Off Peaches' look. Immediately turns on the charm.)* get upset hearing such an honest confession. Don't worry about it, Newt. We'll move the reunion out front under the trees. *(Hugs him.)*

ELSA. Interesting. *(Makes a note.)* Excuse me. I need to step outside and call zee state hospital to check on available beds. *(To Gaynelle.)* Nothing to do vith you, of course. *(Exits into the kitchen.)*

NEWT. *(Enjoys the hug.)* I *knew* you felt the way I do! This feels so — *(Gaynelle pushes him away.)*

GAYNELLE. Shoot me in the head now! Every time I open my mouth I convince that woman I'm totally deranged. She'll probably send me off to Devil's Island.

NEWT. *(Lovesick.)* And I'd be proud to visit you there. That's near Vegas, right?

PEACHES. *(Quickly.)* Come on, Gaynelle. I know you're hot, tired and nervous, but get it together. You can do it! You're a Verdeen! You're strong and —

NEWT. And beautiful and awe-inspirin'. The minute I laid my

eye on you, I wanted to be a better person. That's why I did … *this!*
(Whips off the eye patch.)

GAYNELLE. *(Horrified, screams.)* Ahhh! *(Stops, then.)* You got a new eye!

NEWT. Yeah! I ran right out to Dr. Seymour. You know, "*See More For Less?*" I picked this baby up for a song. And other than falling out now and then, it's a real good fit. *(In love.)* I did it for you.

GAYNELLE. Well, that's … just great. Um … congratulations! *(Slaps him on the back. Newt's eye falls out, he covers the "empty socket" with his hand.)*

NEWT. Dang! There it goes again! Somebody sees that on the floor, it could curl their hair. *(Drops to the floor, searches for the eye.)*

GAYNELLE. *(Snaps to attention.)* Hair?! Oh my God! I never washed the perm solution out of my hair! *(Races out the hallway door.)*

NEWT. *(Watches her leave.)* There goes one fine woman.

PEACHES. *(Flirty, opens her robe to reveal a bit of leg. Stands to one side of Newt so he can't miss it.)* Good news! There's more than *one* in this family.

NEWT. Huh? *(Turns, stares at Peaches' leg.)* Oh! *(Scrutinizes the leg.)* Ohhh. Know what? Mama found her a real good cream on the TV that fixed her unsightly spider veins just like *yours!* Want me to see if there's any of it left?

PEACHES. *(Deflated.)* No thanks. Look, just go give the A.C. another try.

NEWT. Okey-doke, but no promises. Hey, found it! *(Picks up his eyeball.)* Slippery little devil! Maybe I shoulda bought me the next size up. *(Exits the front door as Jimmie Wyvette, dressed in jeans and a shirt, runs in from the kitchen.)*

JIMMIE WYVETTE. Okay, I'm here. Just point me at what needs to be done!

PEACHES. Which would be *everything!* We've got to get this place pulled together and move all my stuff out of Grover's RV. Where have you been?!

JIMMIE WYVETTE. Workin' for the team! I figured I'd bike over to LaMerle's so she wouldn't see my car, get into her crawl space, pull her fuses so she can't bake her cake. She loses, Gaynelle wins. Brilliant, right? So, I try to sneak past the porch, but she's waitin' in her rocker, holding that rifle of hers. Says she's taking precautions against any funny business that might have a *negative impact on her ultimate victory this afternoon.* Can you believe that woman's trust issues?

PEACHES. You can't be doing undercover operations alone! You'll just make things worse. Now, control yourself. What's wrong with you?

JIMMIE WYVETTE. I dunno. Ever since we got out of jail, I've felt jumpy. Gettin' a taste of a life of crime can screw with your head. I kinda like flirtin' with the dark side. Which is probably the reason I stopped by Bitsy's like I did.

PEACHES. Maybe I don't want to hear this.

JIMMIE WYVETTE. Too late. I'm on a roll. See, I snuck into Bitsy's and stole one shoe from every pair she had in her closet. Guess *barefoot Bitsy* won't *be bothering Burton* today. *(Laughs victoriously.)* 'Cause if she tried, she'd look a fool. *(Gaynelle reenters from the hallway door. Her hair is a big, crisp ball of frizz.)*

GAYNELLE. *(Rails.)* This is your fault, Peaches! You told me you didn't have time to fix my hair, so I did it myself and now … now every Verdeen's going to be convinced I'm crazier than a vegetarian at a pig pickin'! *(To Jimmie Wyvette.)* And if it weren't for *you*, we wouldn't have spent the night in jail.

JIMMIE WYVETTE. So that's the thanks I get for trying to help save your house?

PEACHES. Can we just put a pin in that for now? *(Pointedly.)* We've got a *psychological evaluation* going on!

JIMMIE WYVETTE. Not my problem! I'm not the *nut job!* Gaynelle is.

GAYNELLE. Don't you call me that! *(Swats Jimmie Wyvette on the butt.)*

JIMMIE WYVETTE. I just call it like I see it! *(Swats Gaynelle on the butt.)*

PEACHES. You can't talk ugly to Gaynelle! *(Swats Jimmie Wyvette on the butt.)*

JIMMIE WYVETTE. Stop it! *(They rotate in a circle, swat each other's behinds.)*

PEACHES. No, you stop it!

GAYNELLE. No, *you* stop it!

JIMMIE WYVETTE. No, *you* — *(Elsa reenters from the kitchen. Watches a moment. The cousins realize she's there and stop. Beat.)*

ELSA. Thees explanation ees going to be a humdinger.

PEACHES. Well … once again Gaynelle to the rescue. When I

accidentally shoved a fork into the electrical outlet, she knocked me to the floor and saved my life! She's suffered a shock, but that's our girl! Sane *and* safety conscious.

JIMMIE WYVETTE. Yeah. *(Pats down Gaynelle's back and butt.)* She was smokin' a little. But she's good to go now.

ELSA. *(Laughs. Then, stops.)* I do not believe zat for one second. But you *are* making my job easier. *(Makes a note.)* Now, I tink I'll cool off with a glass of iced tea. So, don't do anything vacko 'til I get back! *(Laughs, exits into the kitchen.)*

GAYNELLE. Well, this couldn't be going any worse. All I need now is the IRS to schedule an audit. *(Starts to laugh.)*

JIMMIE WYVETTE. *(Earnest.)* Don't laugh at the IRS, Gaynelle. You never know when they're listening. *(Glances around suspiciously.)*

GAYNELLE. Face it, this evaluation *and* the reunion both have disaster written all over them. Now I know how people on the *Titanic* felt! Break out the champagne! I'm going down! *(Laughs.)*

PEACHES. Well, as long as you're slap-happy, I may as well tell you, Audra Crump called. She was drivin' her singin' birds back from a gig in Flatonia and a yellow jacket got into her van and stung her so bad, she drove right into Bland Lake. *(Gaynelle laughs harder, Jimmie Wyvette gets tickled.)* And Audra's so swollen, she can't fit into any clothes. We can't have a fat, naked bird lady at the reunion. Half the Verdeens are Baptists! *(Gaynelle and Jimmie Wyvette howl.)* Come on, you two. Elsa's in the kitchen, get a grip! *(Newt sticks his head in the front door.)*

NEWT. Mind if I use your hose to wash off my eyeball? It rolled through some *squirrel poop* out in the yard. *(Beat. All three women erupt in laughter. He shrugs, exits.)*

PEACHES. This is just pure-dee exhaustion. Girls, we have to calm down. We cannot have any more hysterics in this house. *(Bitsy storms in the front door, walks unevenly in one high heel and one fuzzy bedroom slipper.)*

BITSY. I'm out in this heat, chasin' my butt-naked mama who's trailing through the neighborhood with my bottle of schnapps, which I keep strictly for medicinal purposes, and I have to put up with your shenanigans, too?! Now, I've tried to be nice, but this is the end of it, Jimmie Wy! You stay away from *my* house, *my* closet and *my* man! And you can kiss your bicycle goodbye 'cause I threw it on the back of Tyncey Crowder's junk truck when he drove past. And there's nothing you can do about it, Miss Unibrow! *(Yells out the front door.)* Mama Doll, for the last time, get you a glass! You're gettin' lipstick all over the bottle! *(Exits.)* 𝖲𝗁𝗎𝗍𝗌 𝖽𝗈𝗈𝗋

JIMMIE WYVETTE. *(Rails.)* Miss Goody One-Shoe! I'll clobber her! *(Jimmie Wyvette lunges after her. Gaynelle and Peaches hold her back.)*

PEACHES. Will you stop trying to murder Bitsy? Listen, I've just had an idea that could give you the edge over her, but we've got to work fast!

JIMMIE WYVETTE. I'll do whatever it takes to put that man-hungry buzzard in her place *(They race out the hallway door. Elsa enters from the kitchen with her iced tea, absorbed in her notebook. Newt enters the front door, eyeball in hand.)*

NEWT. Gaynelle, you have any Krazy Glue? I'm gonna fix this thing once and for all. *(Gaynelle quickly crosses to Newt.)*

GAYNELLE. *(Low.)* Newt, you up for trying something?

NEWT. Well, I'm not that experienced, but I'm open-minded *and* double-jointed.

GAYNELLE. *(Closer.)* Then, I want you to do something you rarely hear a woman ask a man to do.

NEWT. *(Excited.)* Oh, boy! Whatever you got in mind, the answer's "yes!"

GAYNELLE. Good. Go over there and flirt with *(Re: Elsa.)* her.

NEWT. What?! But that wouldn't be honorable, what with my feelings for *you.*

GAYNELLE. I am a desperate woman! Two dozen surly relatives are about to descend on me, this house is hotter than hell fire and if you can't get that woman off me, I'm going to snap! So, turn on the charm, Newt. Make her forget about everything but you.

NEWT. Uh … well … okay. If that's what you want. Yes, ma'am! I'm on it!

GAYNELLE. Great! Now, I've got to get dressed and do something with this hair. Remember, be charming and romantic! *(Exits out the hallway. Newt smoothes his hair, tucks in his shirt, walks straight to Elsa. She looks up. He is in her face.)*

ELSA. *(Beat.)* Somesink I can do for you?

NEWT. *(His version of sexy.)* And how. My name's Newt. *(Puts his hand around her waist and pulls her to him.)* Wanna see my eyeball? *(Blackout.)*

Wednesday

Scene 3

A few hours later. Lights up downstage right on Gaynelle's "front porch." LaMerle, in a church dress, and Aubrey, in a jacket, tie and oxygen cannula, face the audience as they survey "relatives" who've come to the family reunion.

LA MERLE. *(Fans herself.)* Hard to believe these people are Verdeens! Gallivanting around in this heat like heathens, wearing flip-flops, pitching horseshoes, and gossiping like Methodists! Disgraceful! Pitiful shame to think we've come to this.

AUBREY. Yeah, don't the fools realize they *could* be crammed into that fellowship hall at Anointed Word, sufferin' through your endless, yearly blessin' of the food?

LA MERLE. *(Studies him with distaste.)* How quickly the worm turns. Well, unlike this smackdown, my reunions are perfectly organized and run like clockwork. But look at us. Squattin' out here like a pack of porch hounds waiting for our dinner where Lord-knows-who-all can drive by and see us! *(They wave happily at a "passing car," then drop it.)* And if this hog-callin' wasn't bad enough, a high-pressure system's moving in. That sky's yellow as a bucket of corn. Never a good sign. *(Studies "the sky.")* Yes, sir! You live under these Texas skies long enough, you know when it gets this hot, something bad's a-brewin'.

AUBREY. Sweeten up, you old sourpuss. Beans aside, everybody's having a good time. *(Waves offstage.)* Well, looka here! Purvis *did* make it!

LA MERLE. Twenty will get you forty the trunk of his car is filled with pictures of dead Verdeens he wants to show us. Closest that man ever got to a brainstorm was a slight drizzle. *(Fans.)* What I'd like to know is, why Gaynelle decided to have the reunion out here where it's sweltering.

AUBREY. And what *I'd* like to know is why they call 'em *hemorrhoids* and not *asteroids*. *(Cracks himself up.)*

LA MERLE. *(Stares at him.)* You are a twisted little man. And don't go off tom-cattin' with that old Jezebel next door because

44

you're judging the cakes. *(Pointedly.)* I don't suppose you'd know how Gaynelle got herself that red food coloring, would you?

AUBREY. *(Dodges the question, calls:)* Hey, Purvis! Got any new shots of dead relatives you want to show LaMerle? She's just itchin' to see 'em.

LA MERLE. That does it, Judas. You're walking home. *(Attention caught, yells.)* Udelle! Put that down, mister! You got the *di-bee-tees!* Every cookie you eat's gonna cost you another toe! (Blackout. Lights up on Gaynelle's living room. Two cake carriers sit on the dining table. Peaches talks on the phone as she rushes out of the kitchen with a serving dish of beans in her hands. She wears a short black veil that half-covers her face, a short, tight, sexy black dress, black high heels.)*

PEACHES. I know you're busy, Elwin, *so am I!* But this place is a blast furnace, and if you don't get over here and fix this A.C., we'll have Verdeens bitin' the big one right out there under the crape myrtles! *(Hangs up as Newt enters the front door.)*

NEWT. *(Crosses to her, agitated.)* Hey, Peaches. You seen Gaynelle? I've *got* to talk to her about that foreign woman! *(Takes her in.)* Nice get-up.

PEACHES. Why, thank you. I'm in mourning and could use some … *comfort.*

NEWT. Well, lucky thing your whole family's here to give you their shoulders to cry on. Now, about Gaynelle —

PEACHES. *(Foiled again.)* Forget it. She locked herself in her room. Now, I've got to carve the turkey, slice the ham and dish up Cee Cee's weird leftovers, so could you take Aunt Letha's twice-refried beans out to the table for me? *(Hands him the dish.)* Thanks. *(Slaps him on the back, unknowingly knocks his eye into the beans. Newt stumbles out the front door as Peaches crosses to the hall-way door. Calls.)* Gaynelle! Come out, right now! You *are* the hostess of this shindig, so get out here and *host!*

GAYNELLE. *(Offstage.)* I can't. I look ridiculous. They'll laugh at me!

PEACHES. No, they won't. It's so hot, they probably won't even notice. *(Gaynelle reluctantly enters from the hallway door in a summer dress and the Gospel Jubilee Beehive, Number 603.)* See, there! You look fine.

GAYNELLE. I look like the Bride of Frankenstein after a bar fight. *(Notices Peaches' outfit.)* Oh my God! What are you mourning, the loss of the bottom half of your dress?!

PEACHES. I'll have you know this is the only black dress I own.

GAYNELLE. You work for morticians!

PEACHES. I don't *attend* the funerals, I'm a behind-the-scenes artist! But we've got a worse problem. Once the folks out there finish that last round of horseshoes, the only activities left are back-bitin', blame-layin', and re-openin' old wounds.

GAYNELLE. So, for entertainment we're down to dominoes and my nervous breakdown. Is that what you're telling me?

PEACHES. Well, not to toot my own horn, but I think the family's getting a kick out of Jimmie Wy's makeover. *(Jimmie Wyvette wobbles in from the kitchen in a low-cut dress, fishnet stockings, large hoop earrings and high heels she can barely walk in. Her hair is curled, the unibrow is gone, and she's wearing makeup. She is carrying a bowl.)*

JIMMIE WYVETTE. I'd like to meet the *man* who invented high heels … and whomp him upside the head with one.

GAYNELLE. Wow! A dress, heels and *two* eyebrows?! You look like a woman!

JIMMIE WYVETTE. What's that supposed to mean?

PEACHES. *(To Gaynelle.)* Well, I do get paid to work miracles.

JIMMIE WYVETTE. What's *that* supposed to mean?!

PEACHES. Oh, shut up, you're gorgeous. Now, where have you been *this* time?!

JIMMIE WYVETTE. I went over to Burton's to let him take a gander at the new me. But he wasn't there. And on my way back I stopped to, um, do a little something. Now, stand back! I'm aiming to take this bowl of cousin Ardelia's Cajun kidney beans out to the buffet. *(Lurches awkwardly toward the front door.)*

PEACHES. Then move it! *(Fans under her dress.)* We got to get these people fed. And tell everyone, no dessert 'til *after* the cake judging. *(Jimmie Wyvette exits.)*

GAYNELLE. *(Nervous, hurries to her cake carrier.)* Oh, gosh, the judging. *(Rubs the carrier like a magic lamp.)* Come on, baby. It's all riding on you!

PEACHES. Why would LaMerle trust us enough to leave her cake in here?

GAYNELLE. *(Turns LaMerle's cake carrier around; it's padlocked.)* Trust has nothing to do with it. *(Fans wildly.)* Dang! This wig is frying my brain, my patience is shot and I'm ready to bite the head off the next fool who crosses my path. *(Cousin Purvis enters in*

flashy plaid pants pulled up almost to his armpits.)
PURVIS. *(Too loud.)* I've been looking for you two! *(They freeze.)*
Haven't been avoiding me, have you? *(Loud laugh.)*
PEACHES. Why of course not, cousin Purvis. Seeing you is
always … a treat.
PURVIS. *(Gives Gaynelle a rib-crushing hug.)* How come everyone
out there's talking about how you got dumped and I'm the last to
know? Well, now that you're single again, I'll set you up with one
of my buddies down at the colostomy support group. Talk about
a bunch of guys eager to please.
GAYNELLE. Thanks, Purvis, but I'm sitting it out right now. But
I know for a fact, since Peaches is newly widowed, she's got the *urge*
to jump into the dating scene. *(Peaches shoots her a deadly look.)*
PURVIS. Excellent! I'll tell the boys. Oh, and Peaches, you did a
fine job on Great Aunt Ora Lee. *(Pulls a thick picture wallet from
his pocket.)* And I got some fantastic shots of her at the visitation.
Hey, Gaynelle, want to see 'em?
GAYNELLE. I don't really have the —
PURVIS. *(Finds a picture.)* See there? Her eyeshadow exactly
matched the green in the camouflage casket lining. Of course it
was supposed to be closed casket, so I had to sneak my camera
inside the lid and — *(Offstage scream.)*
PEACHES. What was that?! *(Jimmy Wyvette quickly wobbles in the
front door.)*
JIMMIE WYVETTE. Aunt Nini just found Newt's eyeball in the
twice-refried beans! She fainted and looks for all the world like a
dead woman.
PURVIS. Outta my way! *(Whips a camera out of another pocket,
races to the door, excited.)* I want a picture of *that!* *(Exits.)*
PEACHES. Well, to be fair to Nini, if my food stared back at me,
I'd faint, too.
GAYNELLE. We've got to downplay this so it doesn't give that
psychologist more ammo. Let's distract the family by getting the
ham and turkey on the table. Come on, girls, meat parade!
(Gaynelle and Peaches head for the kitchen.)
JIMMIE WYVETTE. Don't open that door! I've got Trinket tied
up in there!
PEACHES. What?! Do not tell me Burton Pearsol's Great Dane is
in that kitchen!
JIMMIE WYVETTE. Well, Bitsy's supposed to be dog-sitting and I

wanted to mess with her head. So I kidnapped him.

GAYNELLE. Trinket's in the kitchen … WITH ALL THAT MEAT?!

JIMMIE WYVETTE. Didn't think about that. *(All run to the kitchen door, open it, look in and scream.)*

GAYNELLE/PEACHES/JIMMIE WYVETTE. OH MY GOD! *(Exit the kitchen door. Newt runs in the front door, his eye patch on, holding his eyeball.)*

NEWT. *(Calls out.)* Gaynelle? I think I've messed up. That favor you asked, I did it too good! *(Behind him, Elsa slips in the front door, strikes a vampish pose.)*

ELSA. *(Glasses gone, hair loose, the neck of her dress unbuttoned, sing-song.)* Oh, New-ton!

NEWT. *(Terrified.)* Uh-oh. *(Races through the hallway door.)*

ELSA. Come back here, you naughty boy! *(Hurries after him through the hallway door. Gaynelle and Peaches enter from the kitchen in a state of shock.)*

GAYNELLE. *One* dog ate a ham, a turkey and enough curry to feed every farmhand from here to Mineola?! *(Jimmie Wyvette rushes in from the kitchen.)*

JIMMIE WYVETTE. Listen, y'all, while I was putting Trinket out back, I caught Uncle Delmus sneaking him a dip and he said he heard the weather on his car radio. We're going to have a mother-whumping storm on us in no time!

GAYNELLE. Well, that does it! Thanks to you, Jimmie Wyvette, this circus is over! *(Calls.)* We're done, Elsa! You can come take me to the nuthouse now!

PEACHES. Wait! We can still pull this off! Heck, when we were kids we got ourselves into worse jams than this and between the three of us, always figured a way out.

JIMMIE WYVETTE. Yeah, let's just grab anything edible we can find. We'll feed the Verdeens, then get the cake-judging done and run everyone out of here before the storm hits. Elsa's got to be impressed with *that* kind of leadership! *(They race out the kitchen door as Newt, his new eyeball back in place, struggles in through the hallway door and drags in Elsa who clings to him, her arms clamped around his shoulder.)*

NEWT. Will you please get off me, woman?

ELSA. But you have unleashed my passions und I am alive again! My heart vill go on! *(Wraps herself around Newt in a passionate embrace as Peaches hurries out of the kitchen with several opened bags of chips and a giant-sized bottle of ketchup. Stops when she sees Elsa and Newt.)*

PEACHES. What's going on?! *(Newt wriggles out of Elsa's grasp as Jimmie Wyvette exits the kitchen with boxes of cereal and a loaf of bread.)* Hey, lady, I thought you were here to work, not put the moves on the man *I saw first!*

JIMMIE WYVETTE. *(Quickly.)* Peaches, I think you need to remember who Elsa is and how important her evaluation is to Gaynelle.

ELSA. Oh, your cousin's ewaluwation is finished. Her case vas clear after I'd spent only a few hours in zis crazy place. In fact, vatever her condition ees seems to be genetic. *(Holds up her notebook.)* It's all right here. And I zink it vill not do any good to be crying over zee spilt milk. So, zat's over. Ka-put! Now, I take care of somesink I have neglected too long! *(Engulfs Newt in another embrace.)*

PEACHES. You head-shrinkin' hussy! I refuse to stand here and let you — *(Her beeper goes off.)* Oh, no! Not now! *(Runs to the kitchen door.)* Gaynelle! Nettioma just bought the farm! Give me her wig! *(Exits into the kitchen.)*

NEWT. *(Pulls himself free.)* And I'd better run go … see how the storm's coming. *(Races for the door, Elsa on his heels.)*

ELSA. I veel help you, my darlink! *(They fly out the front door.)*

JIMMIE WYVETTE. *(Calls to the kitchen.)* You two quit horsing around and help me get these scraps on the table! *(LaMerle storms in the front door, turns, calls back to "the family.")*

LA MERLE. I'm telling you people I've checked every dish and I'm almost positive there are no more body parts in the beans! *(To Jimmie Wyvette.)* Where's our dinner?! Half the Verdeens out there have keeled over from lack of nourishment and I'm so hungry my stomach thinks my throat's been slit! *(Looks her up and down.)* And I might point out, you've never worn a dress once in your life and you pick *today* to give it a shot?! Did you mug the hooker you stole that get-up from?

JIMMIE WYVETTE. *(Deflates.)* It's the earbobs, isn't it?

LA MERLE. Since all you've served us so far is beans, no wonder you decided to keep us outside. Do you geniuses have any idea how embarrassing this reunion is?

JIMMIE WYVETTE. Oh, come on. It's not *that* bad. *(Just then,*

Peaches pulls Gaynelle headfirst by the hair out of the kitchen, struggling to get to the front door. Gaynelle holds onto the wig for all she's worth, oblivious to LaMerle.)

PEACHES. I mean it, Gaynelle! That wig's got a date with Saint Peter and I need to get it to the funeral home *now*!

GAYNELLE. No, I need it! It's the only hair I have! *(Grips the wig as Peaches pulls her out the front door. Beat. LaMerle turns to Jimmie Wyvette.)*

LA MERLE. I will give you girls ten bucks apiece if you'll change your last name to *anything* but Verdeen. *(Blackout. Lights up on "the front porch," downstage right. Aubrey surveys the reunion.)*

AUBREY. *(Calls.)* Hey, Wheeliss, I just thought of another reason it's good to be old — in a hostage situation, we're likely to be released first! *(Cackles with glee.)* Yeah, I'm so old, my birthstone is *lava. (Cackles.)* I'm so old, my friends in heaven must think I didn't make it! *(Laughs himself into a wheeze. Then:)* I'm a funny old cuss. *(Newt sneaks up behind him.)*

NEWT. Hey, Aubrey, I got female trouble. Can you give me some advice?

AUBREY. You bet: Never tell a woman, "Honey, it ain't the *jeans* that make your butt look fat." *(Cackles happily.)*

NEWT. I'm serious. I've got a big problem. The woman I want isn't interested and two women I *don't* want are after me.

AUBREY. Doesn't sound like a problem to me. Just relax and enjoy yourself, son! Speaking of which, come out back and have a smoke with me.

NEWT. I don't smoke.

AUBREY. Want me to teach you how? *(Cracks himself up.)*

ELSA. *(Offstage, sing-song.)* Oh, New-ton!

NEWT. *(Bristles.)* Gotta run! *(Exits.)*

AUBREY. *(Calls after him.)* You know, it's a lot more fun if you let her catch ya! *(Blackout. Lights up on Gaynelle's living room. Jimmie Wyvette works feverishly on LaMerle's cake carrier padlock with a nail file.)*

JIMMIE WYVETTE. Oh, come on! How hard is it to pick a lock? This is our last chance! *(Bitsy, still in two different shoes, explodes through the front door. Jimmie Wyvette jumps, covers and feigns nonchalance.)*

BITSY. *(Snarls.)* I went all over town trying to find Trinket, then I realized the only house I hadn't checked was *this* one. You tried to make me look bad in Burton's eyes, but it didn't work! So, it's time to butt out, you under-handed dog-napper! Burton Pearsol is *mine!*

JIMMIE WYVETTE. *(Temper flares.)* In case you haven't noticed, Burton and me were made for each other. He needs someone he can enjoy the finer things in life with, like NASCAR and goat-ropin', not crochetin' coasters in front of the fire with *you.* Burton Pearsol's *mine!* Period! The end!

BITSY. That rips it! *(Takes a swing at Jimmie Wyvette who ducks, then gets Bitsy into a headlock. They struggle/wrestle/flail around the room with grunts and groans, oblivious to anything else. Newt enters the front door.)*

NEWT. *(To Jimmie Wyvette and Bitsy.)* Could you two get that foreign lady to leave me — Ah, ah — *(Sneezes, his head jerks, his eye is gone. Slaps his hand over the empty socket.)* Well, that's just great! I knew I shoulda gone for that buy two get one free deal! *(Looks for his eye as Cee Cee Windham sneaks in the kitchen door with a box. Newt stops, starstruck.)* Holy cow! Cee Cee Windham, live and in person! My mama was a big fan of yours. She made your butternut squash lasagna every Christmas no matter how hard we tried to stop her. Don't mind me, I'm looking for my eyeball.

CEE CEE. *(To distract him, points across the room.)* Isn't that it over there? *(Newt scrambles to the other side of the room as Cee Cee hurriedly pulls a cake carrier similar to Gaynelle's out of the box, switches it with Gaynelle's. Quickly heads to the kitchen door.)*

NEWT. *(Looks up.)* Naw, that's just a very old olive, but thanks for your help. Say, what's a TV star like yourself doing here anyway?

CEE CEE. Uh … Call it a mission of mercy and say nothing. *(Exits the kitchen door as Jimmie Wyvette and Bitsy wrestle out the hallway door. Elsa immediately enters the front door and strikes a seductive pose.)*

ELSA. *(Sing-song.)* Oh, New-ton! You bad boy. You are so wery hard to catch.

NEWT. *(Panics.)* Well, it's not so much that, ma'am. I was trying to find my new eyeball. Well, see you! *(Drops to his knees, searches under the couch.)*

ELSA. Oh, then I vill help. *(Joins him in front of the couch. Drops to her knees.)* Although, I must say, I find zee eyepatch rather alluring.

NEWT. Huh. You know, you really don't have to help me.

ELSA. I don't mind. I'm havink a vunderful time. I haven't felt thees happy since I vas a girl, twirling my baton in zee drum and bugle corps. *(Newt whips around to her, transfixed.)*

NEWT. *(Instantly sees her in a new light.)* You were a … twirler?

ELSA. Oh, yah! I vas zee chief twirler. *(Seductively.)* My soaring fire baton routine vould make you crazy.

NEWT. *(In love.) You* … you can do the soaring fire baton?! Oh, man, I've always been a fool for a woman who can play with fire.

ELSA. I vould lahf to show eet to you sometime.

NEWT. *(Romantic.)* You bring the baton. I'll bring the matches. *(They kiss as Aubrey enters the front door and continue to make out throughout the scene.)*

AUBREY. Ooh-eee, looka here! *(Re: Newt and Elsa.)* That sure beats the hell outta horseshoes! *(Aubrey cackles as Peaches runs in the front door.)*

PEACHES. *(Oblivious to Newt and Elsa.)* Hope Grover doesn't mind I drove his RV to the funeral home. And I hope y'all don't mind I blocked the driveway.

AUBREY. Oh, I wouldn't worry. Everyone's so hungry, I doubt they have the strength to make it to their cars, much less drive 'em home.

PEACHES. *(Anxious.)* Anything happen while I was gone?

AUBREY. Not much. *(Motions toward Newt and Elsa.)* Just *that.* *(Peaches gasps. Then Jimmie Wyvette and Bitsy wrestle in from the hallway door, Jimmie Wyvette now in the headlock. They wrestle toward the kitchen door and exit.)* And *that. (Gaynelle enters through the hallway door wearing an ornate lampshade on her head.)* And now, *that.*

GAYNELLE. *(Close to jumping off the bridge.)* Don't say a word, Peaches Verdeen Belrose, it's your fault I've been reduced to this. But as God is my witness, I'm going to save my home and prove I'm not crazy.

PEACHES. And wearing a lampshade on your head is just the way to do it. But don't worry, your court-appointed psychologist is kinda busy right now.

GAYNELLE. *(Notices Newt and Elsa.)* Oh, good grief! The woman deciding my fate is necking with *a one-eyed Newt?* It's like I'm just waiting for the next wave of bad news to blow through the door. *(LaMerle storms in the front door.)*

LA MERLE. That's it! I refuse to spend another second out in that broiling oven!

AUBREY. But if you're in here, who's going to keep the crows from stealing all the corn? *(Cracks himself up.)*

LA MERLE. *(Glares at him as Jimmie Wyvette and Bitsy wrestle in from the kitchen and move toward the front door, Bitsy now in the headlock. Then.)* This hootenanny has dragged on long enough! There's a nasty storm brewin', half our family's on the brink of heat stroke, *(Jimmie Wyvette and Bitsy wrestle out the front door.)* fist fights are breaking out. This isn't a family reunion, it's a white trash jamboree! So, let's end this foolishness, Gaynelle, have the cake judging, you deed your house over to me and be done with it.

PEACHES. You *really* want that pound of flesh, don't you?

LA MERLE. A deal's a deal, missy. So, Aubrey, you're gonna pick the best red velvet cake. And if you ever want to taste my King Ranch Chicken again, you better make the right choice. *(Unlocks her cake carrier.)*

GAYNELLE. You're trying to unduly influence the judge!

LA MERLE. Then blindfold the old goat. Nothing I say will make your cake fit for human consumption. It'll only take a bite for him to know mine's the winner.

PEACHES. Fine. *(Snatches a kitchen towel off the table, blindfolds Aubrey.)*

LA MERLE. Well, hurry it up!

AUBREY. Would you just relax, LaMerle? Your butt is clinched so tight, you're creatin' a vacuum. *(Just then, a tornado warning siren begins to wail outside and continues throughout the following. Purvis races in the front door.)*

PURVIS. A twister's touched down on the edge of town. It's comin' right at us!

AUBREY. *(To LaMerle.)* See what you've done with them butt muscles?!

PURVIS. *(Loudly, above the siren.)* I've got the family going around back to the storm cellar. Y'all come on! But if anyone dies during the storm, I got dibs on taking their picture! *(Exits the front door as everyone panics. Blindfolded, Aubrey bumps into walls. Newt and Elsa finally snap to attention.)*

LA MERLE. I'm not going down in that hole with the family! If the twister doesn't get me, the beans will! You're on your own! I'm saving myself! *(Runs out the front door.)*

GAYNELLE. *(Races to the door, calls.)* Stop, LaMerle! You can't outrun it! Oh, no! Peaches, she's taking Grover's RV! *(Wind howls, pushes Gaynelle back.)*

PEACHES. *(Shouts above the wind.)* Let her go! It's between her and the law now. *(Exits out the kitchen door.)*

NEWT. Y'all run get in the cellar! I'll grab Mr. Verdeen! *(Elsa gets to the kitchen door, sizes up Gaynelle.)*

ELSA. *(To Gaynelle.)* Come on, nut job! *(Then.)* I vill be vaiting for you, New-ton! *(Exits the kitchen door.)*

NEWT. *(Rips off Aubrey's blindfold.)* Let's go, Aubrey!

AUBREY. Wait! Grab the cakes, we're half-starved and the sugar rush may take our minds off the fear of death. *(Newt does, hustles Aubrey out the kitchen door.)*

GAYNELLE. Where's Jimmie Wyvette?! *(Jimmie Wyvette and Bitsy wrestle in through the front door.)* This way, girls! Tornado's coming! We've got to get in the storm cellar! *(Jimmie Wyvette and Bitsy snap to attention.)*

JIMMIE WYVETTE/BITSY. *(Scream.)* Burton!

JIMMIE WYVETTE. *(Above the noise.)* I'll save him! *(Pushes Bitsy.)* Outta my way! *(Heads toward the front door. Bitsy grabs her arm.)*

BITSY. *(Yells.)* The heck you will! Burton's mine! *(Bitsy and Jimmie Wyvette resume the fight. This time, Bitsy's in the headlock. They wrestle out the front door into the wind. Gaynelle looks heavenward.)*

GAYNELLE. *(Above the racket.)* Whatever happened to God *bless* Texas?! *(Races out the kitchen door. Blackout.)*

Wednesday

Scene 4

One hour later. Lights up on Gaynelle in her living room. A scarf tightly tied over her frizzy hair, she talks on the telephone.

GAYNELLE. … I'm so glad you're alright, Cee Cee, and what a relief the town's not torn up. The wind over here was so bad, I couldn't get to the cellar. I wedged myself between the fridge and the deep freeze … When were you here? … You didn't! … Wait, you made it with *what?* … Well, bless your heart for trying, but I'm afraid it's a lost cause … *(Newt and Elsa enter from the kitchen. Elsa holds an ice pack on her head.)* just like my freedom. Gotta go, Cee

Cee! *(Hangs up.)* Elsa, I apologize for everything and I don't know what happened to your head, but I'm sorry for that, too, and if you could just give me another —

NEWT. What *happened* was, Elsa tried to peek out the cellar door in all that wind and a lawn chair conked her good. In fact, *(Pointedly.)* she says she *can't remember anything* that's happened *in the last twenty-four hours.*

ELSA. But I veel alvays remember how kind zees gorgeous one-eyed man has been to me. All I know ees I vas supposed to do an ewaluwation and zen zee lights vent out. *(Studies Gaynelle.)* Who are you?

NEWT. *(Jumps on it.)* Why, this is Gaynelle Verdeen Bodeen, the lady you evaluated. You said she's the sanest person you've ever met. I heard you.

ELSA. *(Still in a fog.)* Yes, I zink eet ees coming back to me now.

NEWT. Don't worry, I'll go with you to Judge Wardlow when you make your report and help you remember the details. *(Guides Elsa to the front door. She exits. He turns back and slips Elsa's notebook out of his back pocket into Gaynelle's hands. Winks.)* Here. I think this may be safer with you.

GAYNELLE. *(Relieved, grateful.)* Thank you, Newt. And Elsa better treat you right. You're one in a million. *(Kisses his cheek.)*

NEWT. I can't believe I got me another twirler. And Elsa likes me fine, just the way I am. So, if y'all find my eyeball, keep it. You know, like a souvenir. *(Exits the front door as Peaches and Aubrey enter from the kitchen door. He carries a large bag.)*

AUBREY. Okay, Gaynelle, we just said goodbye to the last of the Verdeens.

GAYNELLE. And I bet they were all griping about the lousy time they had.

PEACHES. Are you kidding? Everyone was saying this was the best family reunion ever! For some reason, those folks got to partying down in that cellar! They were singing, Aubrey taught them how to line dance.

AUBREY. And you should've seen those Verdeens going after that delicious cake of yours. Man, they couldn't get enough, barely touched LaMerle's. Girl, I don't know what you put in it, but I'm here to tell you your cake wins hands down.

GAYNELLE. I did? You mean I won the bet? I saved my house?!

PEACHES. You sure did, shug. That's why we just went over to LaMerle's.

GAYNELLE. To tell her she lost?

AUBREY. Nope. *(Pulls a beautiful quilt out of the bag.)* I believe this belongs to you. *(Gaynelle takes it, hugs it.)*

GAYNELLE. Grandmary's quilt! *(Jimmie Wyvette rushes in the kitchen door.)*

JIMMIE WYVETTE. Y'all! I've got news that'll blow your minds!

GAYNELLE. So have I, cuz!

JIMMIE WYVETTE. Me first. When Bitsy and me got to Burton's, we found out neither one of us ever really had a chance from the get-go. Burton Pearsol has eloped! And you'll never guess who with. *Rabeena Sadler!*

GAYNELLE. Rabeena Sadler?! You mean … *she* cheated on Sumner like he cheated on *me?!* *(Beat.)* That's the best news I've heard in months! *(Off Jimmie Wyvette's look.)* I mean, I'm sorry for *you* … but I'm tickled pink for *me!*

JIMMIE WYVETTE. Naw, I understand and I'm happy for you. I'm also happy Bitsy didn't get Burton, either. But there may be an upside. I ran into Flawney Jernigan and she told me Travis Ponder's wife was just admitted to the hospital with a high fever. Things could be looking up.

PEACHES. *Really?* You know, I always thought Travis was kinda cute.

JIMMIE WYVETTE. Hands off, Hot Lips. I'm staking my claim on *this* one.

PEACHES. Alright, but the next widower after that is *mine!* These curves were meant to be caressed. This trembling body was meant to be —

GAYNELLE/JIMMIE WYVETTE. We know! We know!

GAYNELLE. This horrible day's turned into one of the best of my life! We threw a great reunion, everybody in the family loved my cake and I saved my home, I got a good evaluation and that tacky little red-head gave Sumner the shaft. Can it get any better than this?! *(Grover herds LaMerle, in handcuffs, through the front door. She's in total disarray, chicken feathers in her hair. Grover carries a steering wheel.)*

GROVER. I just want y'all to know I'm arresting your aunt for grand theft auto.

GAYNELLE. Well, I guess it *can!*

LA MERLE. I was simply trying to go home when that twister picked the RV up and deposited me in Tula Boyette's chicken house. You'll regret this, Mister!

GROVER. Kinda like you'll regret stealing my RV and driving it into the eye of a storm. Judge Wardlow's gonna enjoy this one.

JIMMIE WYVETTE. Why, Aunt LaMerle, looks like you've become a blight on the good name of our family.

PEACHES. You finally made it! Welcome to the *lesser Verdeens!*

GAYNELLE. *(Caresses the quilt.)* And since you won't be moving into *my* house, I think you should just lay low 'til the embarrassment blows over … and hope folks find another idiot to talk about.

LA MERLE. This is outrageous! I'm not standing for it!

AUBREY. Don't think you've got much of a choice. You could learn a lesson from these three girls, take what life throws at you and make it work. You always get a stitch in your knickers because you can't accept it when things don't go your way. Roll with the punches, woman. You'll live longer. Like me. *(Cackles.)*

JIMMIE WYVETTE. *(Pulls Gaynelle and Peaches aside, low.)* We might be able to talk Grover out of this if we want to spare LaMerle the shame of going to jail.

PEACHES. *(Exchanges a look with Gaynelle.)* You know, with family, there *are* times to forgive and forget.

GAYNELLE. You're right. *(Beat.)* But this is *not* one of those times! *(Exchanges high-fives with Peaches.)* Book her, Grover!

GROVER. *(Nudges LaMerle toward the front door.)* Come on. Once I get your mug shot and fingerprints, I can start working on *my* claim for stolen property.

LA MERLE. You'll pay for this, Grover Lout. You've had it in for me ever since I busted your britches in Sunday school class! *(Grover and LaMerle exit the front door. The girls squeal and hug each other.)*

PEACHES. Uncle Aubrey, you've been so good to us, is there anything special we can get you for your birthday?

AUBREY. Naw! I've already got the gift I want. *(Just then, Mama Doll enters from the kitchen, a large, bright red bow tied around her chest.)*

MAMA DOLL. Come on, Love Machine! Time's a-wastin'! *(With a squeal, she shuffles toward the front door. Aubrey shuffles after her as fast as he can.)*

AUBREY. I'm hot on your trail, you feisty vixen! *(They exit the front door.)*

GAYNELLE. Alright, girls! Last one under the quilt cleans up after Trinket! *(Runs to the couch, the others follow. They sit. Gaynelle spreads the quilt over them. They pull it up to their chins.)* Ahhhh! This is what I've wanted for so long.

JIMMIE WYVETTE. Just like old times. All that's missing is the cocoa.

PEACHES. Well, it's been a week to remember. But I've got to say, I think our Gaynelle's back *(Mimics Elsa.)* ... and zat's a wery good ting! *(They laugh.)*

GAYNELLE. But I couldn't have done it without you two. And Peaches, you gave up your home to help me save mine, so you're moving in here with me.

PEACHES. Oh, I couldn't do that. *(Then.)* What am I saying? I have nowhere else to go. You're on!

JIMMIE WYVETTE. Well, I don't want to miss out on all the fun. I'm gonna hang out here with you, too. This will be our chance to finally spend more time together like we're always sayin' we will. We'll be laughin', eatin' ... Oh, and speakin' of which, since I didn't get any, Gaynelle, what was in your cake that made everyone so crazy for it?

GAYNELLE. First of all, it wasn't *my* cake. *(Off their looks.)* No, really. Cee Cee told me when she found out I was making Belva Clay's recipe, she knew I couldn't win. Belva Clay never owned up to her *secret ingredient.* But Cee Cee knew what was in it 'cause her mama helped Belva Clay bake cakes for the governor once. So, Cee Cee made Belva Clay's *real* recipe, came over and swapped it with mine. Know what the secret was? Half a bottle of *Kahlua!*

JIMMIE WYVETTE. Of course the Verdeens loved it! That cake was eighty proof! *(They howl.)*

PEACHES. Poor, old LaMerle. Beaten by the demon rum. *(More laughter. Then.)* Oh, isn't it amazing that everything worked out?!

JIMMIE WYVETTE. Yeah. At the very least I thought Gaynelle would do a stretch in the cracker factory.

GAYNELLE. *(Inspired.)* I'm telling you, it's a sign. It's time to straighten up and fly right. Sure, we got lucky today, but from here on out, we're going to be *greater* Verdeens. We'll take the high road. No more weird dramas —

PEACHES. Yeah! No more airing our dirty laundry in public.

JIMMIE WYVETTE. And no more wacky monkeyshines that sets Sweetgum to talkin' about us. Period! *(LaMerle tears in through the front door. Turns back, yells savagely.)*

LA MERLE. I'm not going down without a fight, copper! You'll never put *me* behind bars! *(Flies out the kitchen door, Grover races in after her.)*

GROVER.   Don't make me sic the dogs on you, old lady! *(Sails through the kitchen door after her. The girls look at each other. Beat.)*

GAYNELLE.   Oh, who are we kidding? Why fight destiny? We're Verdeens! *(Jumps up, runs out the kitchen door. Yells.)* We'll help you get her, Grover!

JIMMIE WYVETTE.   *(Runs after her.)* I'll get some rope! *(Exits.)*

PEACHES.   *(Races after them.)* Call for backup! Lots of it! *(Exits. Blackout.)*

The End

PROPERTY LIST

Blank piece of paper
Photo mat, hot glue gun, craft supplies (including heart)
Oxygen tank and cannula
Shopping bag with plate of turnips
Purse
Moon Pie
Boot shine cloth
Small shopping bag
2 bottles of makeup
Large Mason jar with folded slips of paper
2 cups of coffee
Spray can of whipped cream
Purse with manila envelope
Legal document
Clipboards, pens
Beeper
Blonde beehive wig on a foam head
Slice of cake, forks
Tape measure
Blanket
Bouquet of flowers
Bottle of red food coloring
Dirty tarp with "time capsule" containing soggy dirt
Pyrex dish
Screwdriver
Foil-wrapped brick of Velveeta
Soggy paper
Pistol
2 pair of handcuffs
Letter
2 heavy shopping bags
Notebook, pen
Hammer, saw
Glass of iced tea
2 cake carriers with red velvet cake, 1 padlocked
Serving dish of beans

Bowl of kidney beans
Photo wallet with pictures
Camera
Bags of chips
Giant bottle of ketchup
Boxes of cereal
Loaf of bread
Box containing third identical cake carrier
Kitchen towel
Ice pack
Large bag containing large quilt
Steering wheel
Bright red bow

SOUND EFFECTS

Canned music
Beeper
Doorbell
Offstage scream
Tornado warning siren
Wind

NEW PLAYS

★ **AT HOME AT THE ZOO by Edward Albee.** Edward Albee delves deeper into his play THE ZOO STORY by adding a first act, HOMELIFE, which precedes Peter's fateful meeting with Jerry on a park bench in Central Park. "An essential and heartening experience." —*NY Times.* "Darkly comic and thrilling." —*Time Out.* "Genuinely fascinating." —*Journal News.* [2M, 1W] ISBN: 978-0-8222-2317-7

★ **PASSING STRANGE book and lyrics by Stew, music by Stew and Heidi Rodewald, created in collaboration with Annie Dorsen.** A daring musical about a young bohemian that takes you from black middle-class America to Amsterdam, Berlin and beyond on a journey towards personal and artistic authenticity. "Fresh, exuberant, bracingly inventive, bitingly funny, and full of heart." —*NY Times.* "The freshest musical in town!" —*Wall Street Journal.* "Excellent songs and a vulnerable heart." —*Variety.* [4M, 3W] ISBN: 978-0-8222-2400-6

★ **REASONS TO BE PRETTY by Neil LaBute.** Greg really, truly adores his girlfriend, Steph. Unfortunately, he also thinks she has a few physical imperfections, and when he mentions them, all hell breaks loose. "Tight, tense and emotionally true." —*Time Magazine.* "Lively and compulsively watchable." —*The Record.* [2M, 2W] ISBN: 978-0-8222-2394-8

★ **OPUS by Michael Hollinger.** With only a few days to rehearse a grueling Beethoven masterpiece, a world-class string quartet struggles to prepare their highest-profile performance ever—a televised ceremony at the White House. "Intimate, intense and profoundly moving." —*Time Out.* "Worthy of scores of bravissimos." —*BroadwayWorld.com.* [4M, 1W] ISBN: 978-0-8222-2363-4

★ **BECKY SHAW by Gina Gionfriddo.** When an evening calculated to bring happiness takes a dark turn, crisis and comedy ensue in this wickedly funny play that asks what we owe the people we love and the strangers who land on our doorstep. "As engrossing as it is ferociously funny." —*NY Times.* "Gionfriddo is some kind of genius." —*Variety.* [2M, 3W] ISBN: 978-0-8222-2402-0

★ **KICKING A DEAD HORSE by Sam Shepard.** Hobart Struther's horse has just dropped dead. In an eighty-minute monologue, he discusses what path brought him here in the first place, the fate of his marriage, his career, politics and eventually the nature of the universe. "Deeply instinctual and intuitive." —*NY Times.* "The brilliance is in the infinite reverberations Shepard extracts from his simple metaphor." —*TheaterMania.* [1M, 1W] ISBN: 978-0-8222-2336-8

DRAMATISTS PLAY SERVICE, INC.
440 Park Avenue South, New York, NY 10016 212-683-8960 Fax 212-213-1539
postmaster@dramatists.com www.dramatists.com

NEW PLAYS

★ **AUGUST: OSAGE COUNTY by Tracy Letts.** WINNER OF THE 2008 PULITZER PRIZE AND TONY AWARD. When the large Weston family reunites after Dad disappears, their Oklahoma homestead explodes in a maelstrom of repressed truths and unsettling secrets. "Fiercely funny and bitingly sad." –*NY Times.* "Ferociously entertaining." –*Variety.* "A hugely ambitious, highly combustible saga." –*NY Daily News.* [6M, 7W] ISBN: 978-0-8222-2300-9

★ **RUINED by Lynn Nottage.** WINNER OF THE 2009 PULITZER PRIZE. Set in a small mining town in Democratic Republic of Congo, RUINED is a haunting, probing work about the resilience of the human spirit during times of war. "A full-immersion drama of shocking complexity and moral ambiguity." –*Variety.* "Sincere, passionate, courageous." –*Chicago Tribune.* [8M, 4W] ISBN: 978-0-8222-2390-0

★ **GOD OF CARNAGE by Yasmina Reza, translated by Christopher Hampton.** WINNER OF THE 2009 TONY AWARD. A playground altercation between boys brings together their Brooklyn parents, leaving the couples in tatters as the rum flows and tensions explode. "Satisfyingly primitive entertainment." –*NY Times.* "Elegant, acerbic, entertainingly fueled on pure bile." –*Variety.* [2M, 2W] ISBN: 978-0-8222-2399-3

★ **THE SEAFARER by Conor McPherson.** Sharky has returned to Dublin to look after his irascible, aging brother. Old drinking buddies Ivan and Nicky are holed up at the house too, hoping to play some cards. But with the arrival of a stranger from the distant past, the stakes are raised ever higher. "Dark and enthralling Christmas fable." –*NY Times.* "A timeless classic." –*Hollywood Reporter.* [5M] ISBN: 978-0-8222-2284-2

★ **THE NEW CENTURY by Paul Rudnick.** When the playwright is Paul Rudnick, expectations are geared for a play both hilarious and smart, and this provocative and outrageous comedy is no exception. "The one-liners fly like rockets." –*NY Times.* "The funniest playwright around." –*Journal News.* [2M, 3W] ISBN: 978-0-8222-2315-3

★ **SHIPWRECKED! AN ENTERTAINMENT—THE AMAZING ADVENTURES OF LOUIS DE ROUGEMONT (AS TOLD BY HIMSELF) by Donald Margulies.** The amazing story of bravery, survival and celebrity that left nineteenth-century England spellbound. Dare to be whisked away. "A deft, literate narrative." –*LA Times.* "Springs to life like a theatrical pop-up book." –*NY Times.* [2M, 1W] ISBN: 978-0-8222-2341-2

DRAMATISTS PLAY SERVICE, INC.
440 Park Avenue South, New York, NY 10016 212-683-8960 Fax 212-213-1539
postmaster@dramatists.com www.dramatists.com